ÁBŘ. EDVARDA BENEŠE

ŠTEFÁNIKŮV

ČECHŮV

VLTAVA

MÁNESŮV

JOSEFOV

OLD TOWN SQUARE

REVOLUČNÍ

MASARYK STATION

KARLOVA

TÝN CHURCH

LES

STARÉ MĚSTO

HUSOVA

NA

HYBERNSKÁ

PŘÍKOPĚ

WENCESLAS SQU.

MAIN STATION

LEGII

NATIONAL THEATRE

NOVÉ MĚSTO

WILSONOVA

NÁR. MUSEUM

LEGEROVA

VINOHRADY

NEW TOWN HALL

KARLOVO NÁMĚSTÍ

SOKOLSKÁ

SKŮV MOST

JEČNÁ

JUGOSLÁVSKÁ

Prague Pictures

Prague Pictures

Portraits of a City

John Banville

BLOOMSBURY

Excerpts from *Magic Prague* reprinted by
permission of Palgrave Macmillan.

Quotations from *The Trial* reprinted by permission
of Penguin Books. Copyright © Idris Parry, 1994.

Excerpts from *Sudek* by Sonja Bullaty and
Angelo Lomeo reprinted by permission of Clarkson Potter
Publishers, a division of Random House, Inc.
Copyright © 1986 by Sonja Bullaty.

The extracts from Samuel Beckett's translation
of 'Zone' by Apollinaire on page 34 are reprinted
by kind permission of Calder Publications.

The Joseph Brodsky quotation on pages 107–8 is from
Pushkin's Children: Writings on Russia and Russians
by Tatyana Tolstaya, translated by Jamey Gambrell.
Copyright © 2003 by Tatyana Tolstaya. English translation
copyright © 1991, 1992, 1993, 1994, 1996, 1997, 1998,
2000 by Jamey Gambrell. Reprinted by permission
of Houghton Miffin Company. All rights reserved.

The lines from 'The Four Quartets' on page 230 are taken
from *Collected Poems 1909–1952* by T. S. Eliot. Reproduced
by permission of Faber & Faber Ltd and Harcourt Inc.

Published by Bloomsbury, New York and London
Distributed to the trade by Holtzbrinck Publishers

Library of Congress Cataloging-in-Publication Data has
been applied for.

ISBN 1-58234-382-9

First U.S. Edition 2004

10 9 8 7 6 5 4 3 2 1

Typeset by Hewer Text Ltd, Edinburgh
Printed by Clays Ltd, St Ives plc

To Ola Dunham

So much I loved you, though with words alone,
my lovely city, when your cloak was thrown
wide open to reveal your lilac charms;
much more was said by those who carried arms.

– 'To Prague', Jaroslav Seifert,
translated by Ewald Osers

Should we have stayed at home and thought of here?
– 'Questions of Travel', Elizabeth Bishop

Caveat Emptor

This is not a guidebook, nor was meant to be. As to what it is, that is harder to say. A handful of recollections, variations on a theme. An effort to conjure a place by a mingled effort of memory and imagination. A sad song of love to a beloved that can never reciprocate . . . Cities exert a strong, strange fascination, and none is stranger or stronger than the pull of Prague upon the heart of the homesick traveller – sick that is not for his native place, but for the city on the Vltava that he has left behind. Returning there, he feels he has never been away, and yet feels guilty, too, of forgetfulness, neglect, infidelity. Perhaps that is what this is, then, a peace token, a placatory gift tentatively proffered, or just a faithless lover's letter of apology.

I

PERSPECTIVE: SUDEK'S CITY

It was winter the first time I saw Prague, the city blanketed with snow and glistening in the sunlight of an unseasonably bright late January. Perhaps it is the snow that intensifies the silence of the city in these, my earliest memories of it. Prague's silence is more a presence than an absence. The sounds of the traffic, the voices in the streets, the tolling of bells and the chiming of innumerable public clocks, all resonate against the background hush as if against a high, clear pane of glass. There is too in my recollections a sense somehow of incipient flight, of everything in that sparkling scene being poised to slip its tethers and rise up into the dome of brilliant blue: poised, but never to break free. At that time, in the early 1980s, the Cold War was going through one of its decidedly warmer phases, although it was, did we but know it, already beginning to end. I had come to Czechoslovakia in the expectation that all my received ideas of what life was like in Eastern Europe would be overturned. I was to be disappointed – most of the clichés about communist rule would prove dispiritingly accurate – but also strangely exhilarated. Elsewhere is always a surprise.

We had agreed to meet up, J. and G. and I, in Trieste, that melancholy, pearl-grey port where the two women were spending a couple of waterlogged days – Prague's snow was Trieste's slush. The women were eager to get away, and we left on the evening of my arrival, taking the Budapest train and changing at midnight in Ljubljana to the sleeper for Prague. That word, 'sleeper', proved to be a misnomer, for in our carriage of couchettes no one slept, except a large fat man in a shiny pinstriped suit, who snored. At every unpronounceable station along the way the train had to stop and catch its breath, standing in the dark and wheezing like a sick horse. Did we pass through Vienna or did I dream it in a doze? At the Czech border two greatcoated guards with automatic rifles got on board and examined our passports with sceptical frowns, thumbing doggedly back and forth through the pages, searching for something they seemed aggrieved not to find. Their guns looked altogether too square and stubby and ill-designed to be effective, and might have been made of cardboard, but still were frightening. The fat man was hard to wake; at last he sat up blearily and began patting his pockets; producing his papers, he muttered something that made the waiting guards glance at each other briefly and laugh. I rubbed a clear patch on the window and looked out on a bleak expanse of no man's land the size of a football pitch, with ghostly patches of glittering ice, and a watch-tower on stilts, starkly lit, and lamps glowing in the frozen mist like giant dandelion heads, and dim, bundled figures moving spectrally over the countless criss-crossing lines of dully gleaming rail. As I was turning from the window I noticed that someone had blown his nose on the tied-back oatmeal-coloured curtain beside me. The guard who had been inspecting my passport handed it back and in a guttural accent straight out of an old war movie bade me welcome to Czechoslovakia.

Our hotel, the name of which refuses to be recalled, was a large, gaunt cube of concrete and dusty glass on a nondescript street which in subsequent sojourns in the city I have been consistently unable to re-find. It was somewhere not far from Wenceslas Square. The hotel was one of

a not extensive list of such establishments officially approved to accommodate tourists from
the West, all of whom, we had been warned, were
regarded by the authorities as part-time spies, by
illegal money-changers as a costive but surely
inexhaustible source of precious dollars, and
by the young as spoilt playboys and playgirls
who, despite their fabulous and ostentatious
wealth, might be persuaded to take their jeans
off in the street and sell them for handfuls of next
to worthless Czech koruny. And indeed, we had
hardly stepped into the hotel lobby when we were
approached by a broadly smiling young man,
hands jauntily hitched in the high pockets of his
tight leather jacket, who in a curious, crooning
English offered to convert our money at what he
assured us would be 'top-dollar rates, the highest
in town'. In demonstration of the weight of this
offer he quickly flashed a brick-sized block of
koruny – because of that currency's unsayable
abbreviation, *kčs*, we were to give it the nick-
name *kecks* – and as quickly palmed it again into
his pocket. He was the first of many of his kind
that we were to encounter, not dangerous, not
seriously criminal, even, just would-be entrepre-
neurs, immediately recognisable by that professional smile, meant to display innocence and
winning candour, behind which there lurked a

beseeching something that the smile itself could not keep from admitting had small hope of being assuaged. And, to his unsurprised regret, we did decline his services, and passed on with vague apology, feeling uneasily that we might have failed to answer the first distress call directed at us by this bludgeoned, impoverished city. In an alcove, sitting over cold coffee cups at a table under a plastic palm, two achingly beautiful girls in poor imitations of last year's Paris or New York fashions, slim-wristed, pale, with bruise-brown shadows under huge eyes, looked me up and down, flaring their nostrils. Another offer, another regretful no.

For me, bad traveller that I am, there is always a moment of mild panic that comes immediately after the hotel porter has set down my bags, accepted his tip and softly exited from what is suddenly, dismayingly, *my room*. This is the enigma of arrival. How resentful of one's presence this unhumanly neat box seems, the bed hermetically sealed under its mighty bedspread, the chair that no one has ever sat in at the writing table where no one has ever written, that room service menu in its plastic-covered folder, slightly and appetite-killingly tacky to the touch. And how shabby one's poor old suitcase looks, how shamefaced, standing there on the no-colour carpet. Light-headed after that sleepless train journey and buzzing still with travel fever I clambered on to the bed and lay with hands folded on my breast, staring up desperately at the dim ceiling with its sprinkler vents and its miniature, fake chandelier. There was what looked like a wad of chewing gum stuck up there, the legacy of what must have been a prodigiously powerful spitter. Now would be a suitable moment to contemplate a brief history of Prague. Instead, I get up and go down the corridor to talk to J. and G.

Because they are two, they have been allotted a bigger room than mine, a room so vast, indeed, that a thin, chill mist seems to hang in the farther reaches of it. Intimidated by the scale and mortuary stillness of the place, they have not yet unpacked, and J. has not even taken off her coat. We speculate on the possibility of breakfast. The women recount with a shudder an experience at an early-morning buffet in the Gellert in Budapest, when they lifted the lid of a nickel receptacle, unencouragingly suggestive of a kidney-dish, and were confronted with a bloated, grey, semi-circular sausage floating in an inch of warm, greasy water. We wonder if we might go out and look for a café. We are thinking of somewhere small and cosy, as unlike this terrible room as possible, a local place, where locals go, with fogged windows and a copper coffee machine and newspapers on sticks, the kind of place, we know very well, that is never to be found in the vicinity of a hotel such as this one. We have hours to kill before noon, when the Professor is to come and meet us. Despite their hunger pangs the women decide on sleep. I fetch my guidebook and go in search of the river.

I had something more than a visitor's curiosity. Some years previously I had written a novel partly set in Prague at the turn of the seventeenth century. When I was working on the book I did not regard the inventing of a city I had never seen as any more of a challenge than, for example, having to re-create the early 1600s – all fiction is invention, and all novels are historical novels – but I was interested to know what level of verisimilitude, or at least of convincingness, I had achieved. Many readers had complimented me on the accuracy with which my book had 'caught the period', to which I was too grateful and too polite to respond by asking how they could possibly know; I understood that what they were praising was the imaginative feat they felt I had performed in persuading them that this was just how it had been then. But fancy does sometimes summon up the concrete, as anyone who has had a prophetic dream will know. There have been a number of eerie instances when this or that character or happening that I thought entirely my invention subsequently turned out to be historically real. In another novel, set long ago in what is now Poland, I had fashioned – forged, perhaps, would be the better word – a minor character, a soldier, whose presence the plot had demanded, but whose real existence I learned of when, after the book had been published, I received a biographical sketch of him from a helpful Polish historian. The making of fiction is a funny business.

The Charles Bridge was deserted that morning, a thing the latter-day visitor will find hard to credit, since that statued stone span must now be one of the world's most densely peopled spaces, all day long, and throughout most of the night. Frost glittered in the air over the river, just as it had that morning in sixteen-hundred-and-something when my protagonist, the astronomer Johannes Kepler, arrived here from Ulm on a barge, to present the first printed copies of the *Tabulae Rudolphinae* to the Emperor after whom he had so hopefully named his almanac. There, looming above me now as it had loomed above my disembarking astronomer, was the great, blank fortress of Hradčany, and over there

8

was Malá Strana, the Little Quarter, where Kepler would live when he took up his appointment as Rudolf's imperial mathematician. Yes, I had got it right, to a startling degree. Why was I not pleased? In part because, standing there surveying my handiwork, I was struck yet again by the essential fraudulence of fiction. Conjure a winter morning, a river and a castle and a traveller disembarking with a book under his arm, and for the space of a page or two an implied world comes to creaky life. It is all a sleight of the imagination, a vast synecdoche. And yet one goes on doing it, spinning yarns, trying to emulate blind Fate herself.

Much has been written on the beauty of Prague, but I am not sure that beauty is the right word to apply to this mysterious, jumbled, fantastical, absurd city on the Vltava, one of Europe's three capitals of magic – the other two being Turin and Lyon. There is loveliness here, of course, but a loveliness that is excitingly tainted. In his book *Magica Praha*, that ecstatic paean of *amor urbi*, Angelo Maria Ripellino figures the city as a temptress, a wanton, a she-devil. 'The antiquary coquetry with which she pretends to be nothing more than a still life, a silent succession of glories long since past, a dead landscape in a glass ball, only increases her sorcery. She slyly works her way into the soul with spells and enigmas to which she alone holds the key.' Ripellino's Prague is not that miraculously preserved museum piece of noble prospects and Biedermeier frontages which in the Seventies and Eighties of the last century earned some desperately needed hard currency as a backdrop for Hollywood movies set in the never-never time of Mozart and Salieri; his is the city of 'surreptitious passages and infernal alleys . . . still smelling of the Middle Ages,' of cafés and *Kaffeehäuser* – 'in our time,' Kafka writes, 'the catacombs of the Jews' – low dives such as The Poison Inn, The Old Lady, The Three Little Stars, although he does sometimes escape the 'sinister narrowness of those lanes, the stranglehold of those baleful alleys' by fleeing to 'the green islands, the efflorescent districts, the parks, belvederes and gardens that surround Prague on all sides.' This is the old Prague, wistful, secretive, tormented, which survived the communist takeover of 1948, and even the Russian invasion twenty years later, but which, irony of ironies, finally succumbed to the blow delivered to it by a velvet fist in a velvet glove in the revolution of 1989. Now the dollar is everywhere, the young have all the blue jeans they could desire, and there is a McDonald's just off the Charles Bridge.

Well, why not. Praguers have the same right to vulgar consumerism as the rest of us. Freedom is freedom to eat cheap hamburgers as much as it is to publish subversive poetry. Yet one cannot help but wonder what Ripellino, who lectured in Czech literature at the University of Rome and died in 1978, and who tells us how in the dark years he would often go to Germany and gaze longingly eastward, a heartsick lover pining for *die ferne Geliebte*, toward the 'serrated mountain ranges of Bohemia', would have made of the tourist hive that his beloved temptress has turned into. Yet he was a great democrat, loving Prague for her promiscuity as well as for her secretiveness, delightedly citing the grotesque image in Vilém Mrštík's 1893 novel, *Santa Lucia*, of the city reminding the book's protagonist with 'shrill cries that trains were approaching her body and ever new crowds, ever new victims, were disappearing into her infinite womb.'

Ripellino's vast effort of recuperation is an attempt not so much to express the city as to ingest it, to make that metamorphosis of world into self that Rilke tells us is our task on earth. It is analogous to the effort every serious visitor must make. One will not know a city merely by promenading before its sites and sights, *Blue Guide* in hand. Yet how can one know an entity as amorphously elusive as Prague, or any other capital, for that matter? What *is* Prague? Does its essence inhere in the pretty Old Town Square, with its cafés and its famous clock, or, on the far contrary, in the smouldering concrete suburbs, where the majority of Praguers live their decidedly unbohemian lives? Time lays down its layers like strata of rock, the porous limestone of the present over the granite of the communists over the ashes-and-diamonds of the Habsburgs over the basalt of the Přemyslids . . . Where, in what era, may one station oneself to find the best, the truest, view? When I was young I thought that to know a place authentically, to take it to one's heart, one must fall in love there. How many cities have seemed to spread themselves out before me in the very contours of the beloved's limbs. Solipsism. There are as many Pragues as there are eyes to look upon it – more: an infinity of Pragues. Confused and suddenly glum I make my way back toward the hotel. The frost has turned my face to glass.

While we wait, the three of us, in the women's bedroom for the Professor to arrive, we are aware of a faint but definite sense of nervousness, or perhaps it is only an intensity of anticipation. We have come to Prague with a mission. G. has an acquaintance, a young Czech *émigré* recently arrived in New York, I shall call him Miloš. Miloš hopes to study architecture at Columbia, but as yet he has not been able to find a job to support himself while going through college. His father believes he has found a way to help him, by sending him some art works which he will be able to sell for a lot of money. The difficulty is in getting these valuables out of Czechoslovakia. We have volunteered to do it – to smuggle them out. When J. and G. and I were discussing this plan over the international phone lines between Dublin and California it had seemed a bold adventure, but here in the winter light behind the Iron Curtain the inevitable misgivings had begun to assail us. In those days travellers' tales were rife of Western tourists being seized for the most trifling contraband offences and detained for months, for years, even, beyond the help of consular entreaty or ministerial bargaining. While I had often entertained the idle fancy that a jail cell might be the ideal place in which to write, I did not relish the prospect of mouldering for an indefinite period in an Eastern Bloc prison. There rose before me again the image of that Gellert sausage described by J. and G., or a distant relative of it, anyway, all mottled and shrunken with age, and floating not in a nickel dish but plonked down on a rusty tin plate beside a hunk of grey bread . . . Too late to back out now, however, for here was the Professor's hushed tapping at the door.

He was a tall, spare man with pale, short hair brushed neatly across a narrow forehead, a Nordic type unexpected this far to the south and east. Impossible to tell his age; at first sight he might have been anywhere between thirty and sixty. He was handsome, with that unblemished surface and Scandinavian features, yet curiously self-effacing, somehow. Even as he stood before me I found it hard to get him properly into focus, as if a flaw had suddenly developed in the part of my consciousness that has the task of imprinting images upon the memory. I think it was that he had spent so many years trying not to be noticed – by the authorities, by the police, by spies and informers – that a layer of his surface reality had worn away. He had something of the blurred aspect of an actor who has just scrubbed off his make-up. He shook hands with each of us in turn in that grave, elaborate, central European way that makes it seem one is being not greeted for the first time but already being bade farewell. Such a melancholy smile. His English was precise, with only the faintest accent. He welcomed us to Prague in a mild but calmly seigneurial tone, as if it were not Prague we had arrived in but his own private domain. We were to catch this proprietorial note repeatedly here, especially in intellectual circles; so many things that were precious had been taken from the lives of these artists, critics, scholars that they clung to the idea of their city, its history, its shabby magnificence, its unyielding mysteriousness, with the passion of exiles. I had brought a litre of duty-free Irish whiskey as a gift. 'Ah, Jameson!' the Professor said, in the tone of one acknowledging a precious gift from what had seemed a mythic place, silk from Cathay, spices from Samarkand. He took the bottle from my hands delicately, almost tactfully, with a finely judged degree of gratitude. Courtly: that was the word. It struck me I had never met anyone to whom the term could be so aptly applied.

He had advanced no more than a pace or two into the room, and when I moved to shut the door I seemed to detect behind the rimless spectacles that he wore a flicker of unease, of alarm, even. Still holding the whiskey bottle, he stood with his elbows pressed into his sides, his grey raincoat buttoned to the throat. When G. began to speak of the mission that had brought the three of us to Prague he silenced her at once by putting a finger to his lips and pointing to the dusty light fixture in the middle of the ceiling. It was another Prague gesture, always accompanied by a hapless apologetic smile, with which we were to become depressedly familiar. There were, there really were, hidden microphones everywhere.

We went down to the lobby, where the Professor judged that it was safe for us to talk, albeit in guarded murmurs. The two beautiful, black-eyed girls had gone, though their empty coffee cups, the rims printed with smeary lipstick kisses, remained on the table under the plastic palm. There were some twenty pictures, the Professor said, that he wished us to take to his son – not paintings, as I had thought, but photographs, highly valuable original contact prints by a Czech master whose name was unknown to me. The Professor was anxious to assure us that if we had any doubts about taking them out of the country we should say so and he would find another means of getting them to New York. It was perfectly apparent, however, that we were his only hope. No no, we protested stoutly, we were determined to help him. Again that pained, melancholy smile, and he cleared his throat and carefully pressed the tip of a middle finger to the frail gold bridge of his spectacles. In that case, would we do him the honour of coming to dinner that evening at his apartment, where we could not only view the photographs but meet his wife?

At that moment the double doors to the dining room behind us swung open from within, pressed by the backs of a pair of waiters, each bearing a tray piled high with used plates, who spun on their heels in co-ordinated pirouettes like the sleek male dancers in an old-fashioned movie musical, and pranced away in the direction of the kitchens, their trays held effortlessly aloft. In the moment that the doors were open we were afforded a glimpse, peculiarly comprehensive and detailed, of the room's main dining table. It was large and circular, and there were six or eight men seated around it. No doubt my jaundiced memory has exaggerated the look they had of so many pigs busy at a trough. 'Russians,' the Professor said, and sighed. They were raucously drunk, and contemptuously oblivious of the rest of the crowded dining room. I was to see their like again, dozens of them, a couple of years later in Budapest, where I foolishly allowed myself to be persuaded to attend a meeting of the Conference on Security and Co-operation in Europe, a Cold War talking shop now surely defunct. The meeting was supposedly devoted to the encouragement of friendly exchanges between writers from East and West; in fact, most of the time during the sessions was taken up by the Americans and the Russians lobbing insults at each other over the heads of the rest of us irrelevant small-fry. The Soviet delegation were Writers' Union types to a man, grey-faced hacks in sagging suits, smelling of stale cigarette smoke and bad teeth, who during lunch breaks would commandeer the biggest table in the cafetéria and eat and shout and laugh and slap each other on the back in a show of calculatedly ugly triumphalism. Looking back now, of course, I wonder if they, and their counterparts in that Prague dining room, were merely trying to drown out with so much noise the increasingly insistent whisper telling them what they already knew in their heart of unthawable hearts, that it was all coming to an end, the jaunts to pretty satellite capitals, the dachas in the country, the sprees in Moscow's foreign-currency shops, all that passed for privilege in a totalitarian state, all soon to be grabbed by a new élite of mafia chiefs and criminal industrialists and members of this or that President's prodigiously extensive family.[1] But for now the trough was still full, and the Moscow

---

[1] Since I was a delegate, however unwilling, to the CSCE, I feel obliged, in the spirit of fairness, to report that the Americans, while smoother, more soft-spoken, and certainly better dressed than their Eastern Bloc rivals, had been brazenly hypocritical enough to include ostentatiously in their delegation, as a token – apt word – of the racial tolerance and care for indigenous peoples enjoyed in America, a pair of novelists of American Indian heritage. The home of the brave, indeed.

politicos were still snout-deep in it, although the white double doors, swinging in ever more shallow arcs, were shutting them out of our view by two, by two, by two, and the last we saw of them was the fat fellow at the head of the table, his back to us, who in turn was reduced to a large pair of trotters in broad black shoes splayed under a chair, two hitched-up trouser legs, two crumpled grey socks, and the bared lower reaches of two fat, bristled calves, until at last even that much was gone.

The Professor was offering to show us something of Prague. We were grateful, but worried that we might be keeping him from his work, on this weekday morning. He laughed very softly and said that he had all the time in the world. He explained that due to his involvement in Charter 77, the human rights manifesto drawn up at the end of 1976 by dissident intellectuals after the authorities had ordered the arrest of the rock and roll band, Plastic People, he was dismissed from the university, where he had been Professor of Fine Art. Since then, he and his wife had been subsisting on a meagre pension which the State repeatedly threatened to stop if he were to insist on maintaining links with degenerate and anti-revolutionary factions. He knew Václav Havel, of course, still in prison at the time, and often met

his friends from the old days, before 1976 –
before, indeed, 1968 – in cafés and pubs, where
their conversations were monitored by police
informers. He was frequently summoned for
interrogation at police headquarters, even still,
although the authorities must have known that
he was politically powerless. He explained to us,
in tones of weary amusement flecked with bitter-
ness, how the procedure worked. There would be
a phone call early in the morning, often before
dawn, when he was still in bed, and a friendly
voice would ask if he would care to come to such-
and-such a building, always a different one, and
have a chat. Just a chat, the voice would say,
nothing serious, nothing for him to worry about,
he could take his time, there was no hurry, a car
would be outside, waiting for him, when he was
ready. He would get up straight away and pack a
small bag – pyjamas, a clean shirt, change of
underwear, socks, shaving things, the all-impor-
tant toothbrush – while his wife made coffee and
heated rolls. This was their unvarying ritual. It
was strange, he said, but they spoke little on these
occasions, and only of practical things, despite
the fact that they both knew they might never see
each other again. There were friends and ac-
quaintances who had been summoned like this,
'for a chat', and who had not come back. Arrived

at the specified anonymous building in one of the city's more unbeautiful quarters, the Professor told us, he would be placed in a small, windowless room, bare save for a steel table and straight chair, and instructed to fill out a sheaf of official forms, listing the minutiae of his life and the lives of his parents, wife, children, while unseen eyes, as he well knew, watched him through the two-way mirror set before him in the wall. Then the interrogator would stroll in, relaxed, smiling, and infinitely menacing.

These periods of detention, the Professor mildly observed, could be over in half an hour, or might go on for three days and nights, or even longer, with half a dozen interrogators working in shifts. He had never yet suffered physical violence. Like secret police forces everywhere, the Státní Bezpečnost, or StB, had a very great deal of information – when the files were opened after the Velvet Revolution, the names were discovered of tens of thousands of informers on the StB payroll – but found the greatest difficulty in piecing it all together. Frequently, the Professor said, the line of questioning would meander so far from anything or anyone that he might be able to tell them about, even if he were willing to, that he would have no alternative but to fall silent. The interrogators were always nameless.

Many years later, another Czech friend, Zdeněk, a writer and translator, and a leading Charter 77 activist, told me how one day after the fall of the communist régime he was walking in the city centre and spotted on the other side of the street one of his interrogators from the bad old days, and how, before he knew what he was doing, he found himself shouting across the traffic furiously at the fellow, 'What is your *name?* What is your *name?*' as if it were the one most important thing in the world, the one thing that he must know above all. And what did the former interrogator do? I asked, expecting to hear that he had pulled up his coat collar and slunk away in shame. 'Oh,' Zdeněk said with a shrug, 'he smiled, and waved, and called out, *Hello there! How are you?* and went on his way.'

By now we were in Zlatá Ulička – the famous Golden Lane – hard by the walls of the fortress of Hradčany. I do not know how we got there. Indeed, much as I try I cannot remember what means of transport we used in any of our time during that first visit. We must have travelled by bus, or tram, or even, despite J.'s claustrophobia, the metro – still unnervingly spotless, by the way – but I cannot see us on any of those conveyances. We are simply here, and then there, and then somewhere else, with only blank spaces in between. How smoothly does Mnemosyne's magic chariot glide!

Golden Lane is very old, an enclosed, cobbled way blind at both ends. Its tiny houses, clustered against the wall of the Stag Moat, were built at the end of the sixteenth century by the Emperor Rudolf II for his twenty-four castle guards. Why, one wonders, only twenty-four? History's simplest statements have a way of provoking puzzles. In the seventeenth century the houses in Golden Lane were taken over mostly by the city's goldsmiths, hence the name. The curious little street has generated legends, for instance that Rudolf's numerous band of alchemists had their laboratories here – alchemists are a type of goldsmith, after all, which might explain the confusion. It is attractive to think of those magi huddled over their alembics in these cramped little rooms, but my guidebook insists, in a distinctly reproving tone, that despite popular lore, Rudolf's alchemical horde did not work in Zlatá Ulička at all, but were confined to nearby Vikářská Lane, that runs along the north side of St Vitus's Cathedral – yes, yes, we shall visit the cathedral presently. I was more impressed to hear, from the Professor, that Kafka lodged for a time in Zlatá Ulička, at number 22, as did his latter-day fellow-countryman, the great Czech

poet, Jaroslav Seifert.[2] So also, mind you, did the
great Czech fortune teller, Madame de Thèbes,
who lived at number 4 in the years before the
Second World War. More magic . . .

Speaking of Kafka – as how, in Prague, would
one not? – we wondered if it might be possible to
visit his birthplace. Well, yes, the Professor said,
frowning, we could go and look at the house, but
the building, U Věže (At the Tower), originally
owned by the Benedictine order, was burned
down in 1887, some years after the Kafka family
had moved to a new apartment on Wenceslas
Square, and all that remains of the earlier building is the stone portal of the front doorway. A
small carved plaque, by the sculptor Karel Hla-
dík, is attached high up on the wall beside the
door; the memorial was erected in 1965, after the
famous conference on Kafka at Liblice Castle in

[2] Kafka and his favourite sister, Ottla, rented number 22 Zlatá
Ulička in November 1916. Kafka had a room but not, it seems, a
bed; on his days off from the insurance office he would work there
all day, then have his supper, and walk down the Old Castle Steps at
midnight and across the Mánes Bridge to his flat in the Schönborn
Palace in the Old Town. He was happy in Golden Lane: 'it is
something special,' he wrote to his girlfriend Felice Bauer, 'to have
one's own house, to lock the door to the world, not of the room, not
of the flat, but of the house itself; to step out of the door of one's
home straight into the snow of the quiet lane.' Conditions were
primitive, but K. could always improvise. He arrived one day when
the fire was out, he told Ottla, 'But then I took all the newspapers
and manuscripts and, after a while, a very lovely fire was burning.'
All the manuscripts . . .

1963 had made Prague's greatest artist accepta-
ble to the authorities as a critic of decadence and
capitalist alienation. Before that time, the Professor explained, Kafka officially was a non-person
in the Czechoslovak state. The communists did
not stop at suppressing his works, but held that
they and their author had never existed. One
almost has to admire the simplicity of it, the
horrible, blank thoroughness of this erasure of
a life and its darkly luminous products.[3]

We walked on, up the steeply ascending street,
the patches of packed snow squeaking under our
boots. The sounds of the city came to us on this
high hill as a kind of troubled murmur. We had
fallen silent. The thought of Kafka having been
for so long a non-existent presence in his native
city seemed so . . . well, so Kafkaesque, that we
felt abashed. But not as abashed as the Professor
looked. There was in those days among the
decent folk of Prague a particular form of embarrassment in regard to the city's, and the country's, plight, held bound and mute under Soviet
domination and what Ripellino in a finely con-

---

[3] Kafka's attitude to his native city was made up of equal measures
of love and hate. 'Prague doesn't let go,' he wrote to his friend Oskar
Pollak in 1902. 'Either of us. This old crone has claws. We would
have to set it on fire in two places, at Vyšehrad and the Castle; only
then might it be possible for us to get away. Perhaps you'll give it
some consideration before carnival.'

temptuous phrase calls 'the fell tyranny of its Calibans'. It is an affliction that is common, one suspects, to all subjugated people, this tongue-tied, apologetic shame before the eyes of strangers. In Ireland during the catastrophic famines of the 1840s, when the country's condition was desperate – successive rebellions against English rule had failed, the economy was in collapse, the language was as good as dead – whole families of starving countrypeople would turn in upon themselves, shutting and barring the doors of their cabins and blocking out the windows against the world's gaze, and wait for death. It was as if they could not believe that such misfortune were not somehow, at some level, their own fault. I never had the nerve, the effrontery, that first time or on subsequent visits to the city, to ask the Praguers of my acquaintance, or even those who over the years became my friends, whether the Czech people felt deep down that they had somehow failed themselves in 1968, and had not done enough to halt the Soviet tanks in their tracks. But what, really, could they have done? What could they have been expected to do, those petalled children of the Age of Aquarius? *How with this rage shall beauty hold a plea / Whose action is no stronger than a flower?* Shakespeare beautifully, tragically, asks. At the time we all recalled the Hungarian uprising of no more than a dozen years previously, the bodies in the streets, the rubble, the ruined city. Who could have wished a like fate for Prague?

In what was no doubt an attempt to dissipate the gloom that had settled on us, and to demonstrate that the city had its living writers, whose flesh-and-blood reality the authorities could not deny, the Professor took us to lunch at a literary pub. At least, that is how he described it. Hidden in a narrow, twisting street somewhere between the Old Town Square and the river, it was a long, low, brownish place with benches and three-legged stools and a kippered ceiling – was it the fabled *U Zlatého Tygra*, The Golden Tiger? – a Bohemian version, I immediately thought, of Mulligan's pub in Poolbeg Street in Dublin. *U Zlatého Tygra*, if such it was, that day was riotously busy. Shirt-sleeved barmen were slinging litre-sized steins of Pilsner, while simultaneously dealing out piled mounds of sausage and potatoes to clamouring customers on all sides. Watching these professionally dour masters ply their trade was like witnessing a troupe of acrobatic conjurors at work with sticks and spinning plates. The air was dense with steam and cigarette smoke, and in the stippled, misted mirrors the waiters' ghostly doubles darted. We asked the Professor to point out the best, or at least the best-known, writers; we were hoping for a Hrabal or a Škrovecký. The Professor looked about carefully, then coughed, and once again touched a fingertip to the bridge of his spectacles, that gesture which I knew by now was the prelude to an apology. The literati, it seemed, were not much in evidence today. That fellow by the window, the one in the scarf, styled himself a novelist, but he had never published anything, and no one had yet been permitted to read his work. The woman in the corner, a handsome blonde *d'un certain age*, was rumoured to have had an affair with Seifert. That haughty-looking chap with the cockerel's crest of silver hair had been engaged for twenty years on a Czech translation of *Finnegans Wake*, and was known to be a police informer. And there, glaring at him across the room, was sad old Svoboda, the critic and feuilletonist, whose name had not been allowed to appear in print since '68. I told the Professor there was no need for him to apologise; in Dublin in the early Sixties, when giants still walked the earth, I would often venture into McDaid's or the Palace Bar or Mulligan's, hoping for a glimpse of Brendan Behan or Patrick Kavanagh, but there never seemed to be anyone there except other haunted-eyed neophytes such as I was, and the odd penniless poetaster hoping to cadge a drink. The Professor wanly smiled. I could see he did not believe me, thought I was merely being kind. Life, as Kundera's title has it, is elsewhere.

Lunch. Ah. Perhaps this is the place to say a word about Czech cuisine; a word, and then on to more appetising topics. My Czech friends, whom I value dearly and would not wish to offend, should skip smartly the next two paragraphs – you have been warned. I have eaten badly in many parts of the world. There is a certain plate of macaroni studded with gobbets of cow's kidney that was served to me by a resentful cook – her name was Miss Grub; honestly, it was – at a friend's house in London many years ago which I shall never forget. At a hostelry in a pleasant little town not far from Budapest I have been confronted by a steaming platter of sliced goose, mashed potato, and sauerkraut, three shades of glistening grey. And what about that inoffensive-looking green salad which I ate without a second thought in a little lunch place off the tourist trail one glorious autumn afternoon in Oaxaca, which infiltrated into my digestive system a bacillus, busy as a Mexican jumping bean, which was to cling to the inner lining of my intestines for three long, queasy and intermittently galvanised months? I do not say that my culinary adventures in Prague were as awful as these. Indeed, I have had some fine meals there over the years. In general, however, it must be said, and I must say it, that the Czech cuisine is, well, no better than that of Bavaria, which statement is, as anyone who knows Bavaria will confirm, a ringing denunciation. I recall an evening at a *Bierkeller* in Regensburg where . . . but no, that is another story, and another town.[4]

Both the Czechs and the Bavarians, close neighbours that they are, have in common an inexplicable but almost universal enthusiasm for . . . dumplings. These delicacies can be anything from the size of a stout marble – what in my childhood we called a knuckler – to that of a worn-out, soggy tennis ball, with which they share something of their texture, and possibly of their taste. The Czech species comes in a broad variety of strains, from the very common *houskové knedlíky*, or bread dumplings, through the *bramborové knedlíky*, potato dumplings, often

---

[4] But I cannot refrain from reproducing the description of a dish I found on a menu in the Kepler Beer Restaurant in the Czech town of Kutná Hora not long ago: 'Filled chicken brest (sic) with banana in almond sauce with cream and griotce.' Serve me right for asking for an English-language menu. Griotce, by the way, is a cherry liqueur; I have never, so far as I know, tasted it.

temptingly served alongside a smoking midden of white sauerkraut, to the relatively rare – rare in my experience, anyway – *ovocné knedlíky*, or fruit dumplings. Perhaps the dumpling's most striking characteristic is its extreme viscosity. It sits there on the plate, pale, tumorous and hot, daring you to take your knife to it, and, when you do, clinging to the steel with a kind of gummy amorousness, the wound making a sucking, smacking sound and closing on itself as soon as the blade has passed through. Dumplings can be served as an accompaniment to anything, whether the lowly *párky*, or hot dogs, or the mighty slab of *svíčková*, boiled fillet of beef. They can have their own accompaniments, too, for instance the creamy, sour-sweet sauce called *smetaně*.[5] That day at The Golden Tiger, if that is where it was, we stuck to simple fare: plates of only slightly worrying *klóbasy* – grilled sausages – and dark bread, heavy but good, washed down with bubbling beakers of glorious Czech beer, which tastes of hayfields baking in summer heat. But there would be other mealtimes, oh, there would, from which memory averts its gaze . . .

After lunch we thought we might visit a gallery

[5] Another question not to be asked: does it strike the Czech ear oddly that one of their great national composers should be called Smetana, which means cream? But then, think of the Russians: '*pasternak*', I am told, in English is 'parsnip'.

or two; G. worked at the San Francisco Museum of Modern Art, and was eager to see the local treasures. Again a faint cough from the Professor, again the fingertip to the spectacles. The main museums – including, if I remember rightly, the National Gallery – were shut, he told us, and had been since sometime back in the Seventies. No reason had been given for their closure, and enquiries to the 'faceless authorities' – in Prague, the cliché took on a fresh, or rancid, rather, new life – elicited either a contemptuous silence, or pompously worded, but carefully vague, assurances that elaborate programmes of repair and refurbishment were about to get under way. As yet, however, there had been no sign of these promised initiatives, and the Professor and his fellow scholars were becomingly increasingly alarmed as to the condition of the sequestered art works, which had not been tended to for nearly a decade.

In place of a museum, the Professor offered to show us St Vitus's Cathedral. We climbed to the hill of Hradčany once more, labouring up the shallow granite steps, 'each one the width of four bodies laid head to foot,' the novelist Gustav Meyrink notes in his accustomed cheery fashion. The sun was gone now, and a sky bearing a bellyful of snow loured over the afternoon.

The great church reared above us, 'ornate and mad', in Philip Larkin's fine description of churches in general, like a vast, spired ship run aground and sunk here in the midst of the castle complex, clamoured about on all sides by the reefs of Baroque palaces, coral-coloured. The cathedral is yet another of the gifts lavished on Prague by the munificent Charles IV. Work began on it in 1344, and was not completed until 1929, if such a building can ever be said to be finished. The first architect was Matthew of Arras. Here is the Golden Portal, held aloft on the delicate webbing of Peter Parléř's three Gothic arches. When one looks up, the entire building seems to be speeding massively through the brumous air, going nowhere. See the gargoyles, 'these caricatures, these apings-at', as Rilke, another of Prague's unwilling sons, has it; I always feel a pang of pity for gargoyles. In 'View from the Charles Bridge', Seifert writes:

> *There are days when the Castle*
> *and its Cathedral*
> *are gloomily magnificent,*
> *when it seems*
> *they were built of dismal rock*
> *brought back from the Moon.*

We enter into a huge, reverberant silence, shadowed, ancient air. The rose window above us
dimly glows, feeding upon the wan winter light;
the stained glass, I silently observe, is distinctly
gaudy. In 'Zone', the poet Apollinaire, 'montant
au Hradchin', experienced here a moment of
Modernist dread:

> Épouvanté tu te vois dessiné dans les agates
> de Saint-Vit
> Tu étais triste à mourir le jou où tu t'y vis
> Tu ressembles au Lazare affolé par le jour

Which Samuel Beckett renders as:

> Appalled you see your image in the agates of
> Saint Vitus
> That day you were fit to die with sadness
> You look like Lazarus frantic in the daylight

My footsteps ring on the floor of the nave and
fetch back reproachful echoes. I enter St Wenceslas's Chapel, into which one could wander freely
then but which nowadays is barred to the public
by a velvet rope, international tourism's ubiquitous, polite but unvaultable hurdle. Buried in this
chapel is Wenceslas I, that hymned good king,
fourth Přemyslid ruler to hold the throne, supposedly assassinated on this holy ground at the
behest of his bad brother Boleslav in or about

935. The interior walls, so my guidebook tells me,
are studded on their lower levels with '*c*.1372'
precious stones; I am impressed by that laconic '*c*'.
On the north door of the Wenceslas Chapel there
is a bronze ring, gripped firmly in the mouth of
what I am told is a lion,[6] to which the dying king is
said to have clung as the assassins struck.

I am always surprised to think that churches
should be considered places of comfort and
sanctuary. On the contrary, they seem to me,
especially the big, Catholic ones, soulless memorials of anguished atonement and blood rites,
gaunt, unwarmed and unwelcoming, heavy with
Wallace Stevens's 'holy hush of ancient sacrifice'.
Years ago, in Salisbury Cathedral, eavesdropping
one twilit eve on the cathedral choir at rehearsal,
I was appalled to notice that beside me my seven-
year-old son was weeping silently in terror. As I
tried to comfort him I looked about – I, who was
compelled by a devout mother to spend extended
stretches of my childhood in places such as this –
and saw it all suddenly from the perspective of a
little boy born to godless parents: the grimacing

[6] But which looks to me more like a cheerful if not over-bright dog,
like the dog of St Wenceslas which the short-story writer Jan Neruda
says is depicted in a painting behind the cathedral's main altar,
although I could not find it. And anyway, according to the history
books, Wenceslas wasn't murdered in St Vitus's, or even in Prague,
but in a town outside the city, Stará Boleslav.

statues, the cross-eyed martyrs in stained glass, the shot-torn regimental banners, the maniacally carved pulpit, all quite mad – Larkin was right – and hideously menacing. What frightened my son most, he later confessed, were the *sotto voce* comments and encouragements that the choir master breathed into his microphone in the pauses between verses; they must have sounded like the celestial chidings of weary, terrible old Yahweh himself.

Yet it occurs to me that a few centuries ago my son in that place would not have been frightened at all, only awed, and dazzled, too. We easily forget that ours is a world permanently lit, that we live in a garish, practically nightless present in which our senses are assailed from all sides, by small flickering screens and huge advertisement hoardings, by public music, by a myriad perfumes, by the textures under our hands of rich stuffs and polished hides. The world out of which this cathedral grew was another place entirely. In the opening pages of *The Autumn of the Middle Ages*, Johan Huizinga writes:

When the world was half a thousand years younger all events had much sharper outlines than now. The distance between sadness and joy, between good and bad fortune, seemed to be much greater than

for us; every experience had that degree of direct-
ness and absoluteness that joy and sadness still have
in the mind of a child ... Just as the contrast
between summer and winter was stronger then than
in our present lives, so was the difference between
the light and dark, quiet and noise. The modern city
hardly knows pure darkness or true silence any
more, nor does it know the effect of a single small
light or that of a lonely distant shout.

What an aspirant marvel St Vitus's must have
been long ago, with its Golden Portal glowing, its
great doors flung open and its rose window angling down God's celestial light. The colour, the
sonorities, the incense, the thousand candles burning. And the bells. Huizinga again: 'The bells acted
in daily life like concerned good spirits who, with
their familiar voices, proclaimed sadness or joy,
calm or unrest, assembly or exhortation.'

'Churches,' Ripellino remarks, smacking his
lips almost audibly, 'exert a fatal attraction on
Prague fiction's morbid characters.' A key scene in
Meyrink's ghastly and sometimes risible novel
The Golem takes place in St Vitus's Cathedral,
amid the 'enervating smell of tapers and incense'.[7]

---

[7] This is the phrase as translated in Ripellino/Marinelli's *Magic
Prague*; Gustav Meyrink's *The Golem* is available in a somewhat
capricious English translation by Mike Mitchell (London, 1995).

Even the commonsensical Jan Neruda, chronicler of the doings of the simple folk of Malá Strana, feels drawn to that grey stone eminence on the hill, where within its fastness he in his turn detects that not so enervating but no less 'distinctive combination of incense and mould found in every house of worship'. In Neruda's story 'The St Wenceslas Mass', the narrator recalls how when he was an altar boy, he and his friends knew for a fact that St Wenceslas returned every night at the stroke of midnight – when else? – to celebrate Mass at the cathedral's high altar. One night he hid himself in the locked cathedral, determined to witness the saint return to enact the ghostly ceremony. As the last faint glimmer of evening fades and night comes on, and 'a silvery, gossamerlike radiance floated over the nave,' the boy is seized with a numinous terror: 'I felt the entire burden of the hour and of the cold, and suddenly I was overcome by a vague – yet for its vagueness all the more shattering – terror. I did not know what I feared, yet fear I did, and my weak, childlike mind was powerless to resist.'

Prague writers love to frighten themselves, especially the decadents of the late nineteenth and early twentieth centuries. They revel in the uncanny. Their fiction, according to Ripellino, 'is characterised by an oppressive recurrence of the

Spanish-derived image of the crucifix [Habsburg emperors of the sixteenth and seventeenth century, including Rudolf, were schooled by Spanish Jesuits], a gloomy tangle of wounds and rent limbs, a fountain of gushing blood, a spiritualist vision and source of terror'. He gives a skin-crawlingly vivid example from the unlikely-sounding *Román Manfreda Macmillena* (*The Novel of Manfred Macmillen*, 1907) by Jiří Karásek ze Lvovic:

> No sooner did my eyes fix on the cross hanging on the wall than I felt behind me the presence of a living being. I was seized by terror, for now even the cross at which I had been gazing assumed a ghostly appearance: it was no longer hanging on the wall but suspended in the darkness.

In another tale, *Gotická duše* (*A Gothic Soul*, 1905), the 'large Christ covered with bleeding wounds that glowed in the darkness like mystical signs descended from the arms of the cross and slowly approached the altar'.

Of course, the most famous literary visit to St Vitus's takes place in *The Trial*, when Josef K. is charged, by his employer at the bank where he works, with showing a visiting Italian business-man the artistic sights of the city. The Italian, with his nervous laugh and steel-grey bushy moustache – one would surely describe him as sinister except that there is nothing in this novel that is not sinister – is pressed for time and opts to restrict his viewing to the cathedral. It is all a cruel ruse, anyway; the Italian does not turn up, and Josef K. is left to loiter uneasily in the echoing nave as the morning steadily, eerily, darkens, encountering 'the silver sheen of a saint's figure', no doubt the same 'silver St John' of Nepomuk identified by the boy in Jan Neruda's story. Josef K. cannot account for the strange atmospherics that are affecting the daylight. 'What sort of weather could there be outside? It was not just a dreary day any more, it was the depth of night.'

In the distance a large triangle of candle flames flickered on the high altar. K. could not have said with certainty whether he had seen them earlier on. Perhaps they had just been lit. Vergers are stealthy by profession and are scarcely noticed. When K. happened to turn round he saw not far behind him a tall thick candle also alight, this time fixed to a pillar. However beautiful it looked, it was quite inadequate to illuminate the altarpieces which mostly hung in the gloom of the side-chapels; it only made the darkness more intense.

The scene is set for K.'s encounter with the priest, who claims to be a prison chaplain – *the* prison chaplain, in fact – who knows Josef K.'s name, and who tells him the terrifying parable of 'the man from the country' who comes seeking 'entry into the law' but is prevented by the implacable door-keeper, who makes him sit by the door for years, until the man grows old, and reaches the threshold of death. 'You are insatiable,' the door-keeper tells him.

'But everybody strives for the law,' says the man. 'How is it that in all these years nobody except myself has asked for admittance?' The door-keeper realises the man has reached the end of his life and, to penetrate his imperfect hearing, he roars at him: 'Nobody else could gain admittance here, this entrance was meant only for you. I shall now go and close it.'

In his lengthy exegesis on the implications and possible meaning of the parable, the priest observes that 'right at the beginning [the door-keeper] plays a joke on the man by inviting him to enter in spite of the express and strictly enforced prohibition . . .' We know that Kafka had a sly and mordant sense of humour. Of his job as an insurance assessor giving judgement on workers' claims he exclaimed in a letter to his friend Max Brod how extraordinarily accident-prone the world seemed to be, and how 'one gets a headache from all these young girls in the porcelain factories who are forever throwing themselves downstairs with mountains of dishes'. There is also the anecdote which tells of him beginning to read from *The Trial* to a gathering of friends, but collapsing into such laughter on the first page that he had to abandon the reading. The 'joke' in the parable of the law, however, is, as Mark Twain said of German humour, no laughing matter. A few years ago, not long before his death, the great Germanist and Kafka scholar, Eduard Goldstücker, described to me how he and other loyal communists in Prague were rounded up in December 1951 at the beginning of a new wave of Stalinist show trials. When he asked to know why he had been arrested, the answer came with an ironic smile: 'That is what *you* must tell *us.*' I immediately thought of the prison chaplain speaking to Josef K. of the door-keeper's friendliness and humour, and even compassion. I thought as well of the two gentlemen in frock coats, with the air of broken-down actors, pale and fat and wearing top hats, 'apparently the non-collapsible kind', who come to K.'s apartment on the eve of his thirty-first birthday to fetch him away to his execution in the little quarry in what is most likely the Strahov district of the city. 'There was nothing heroic in resisting, in making difficulties for the gentlemen now, in putting up a defence at this point in an effort to enjoy a final glimmer of life.' . . .

All at once I was cold; an empty cathedral is a chilly place. The Professor was standing a little way off with J. and G., pointing upward to one of the stained-glass windows and explaining some fine detail of the depicted scene. Now, suddenly, and at no particular prompting, it was my turn to feel embarrassed. As I looked at him there, in his shabby raincoat, with his pale, thin hair, the high, Slavic cheekbones, those touchingly inoffensive spectacles, I asked myself what did I know of the difficulties of this man's life, of the stratagems he had been compelled to engage in over the years in order to preserve dignity and self-respect, or in order simply to feed and clothe himself and his wife and son. My friend Zdeněk had made a Czech version of *Hamlet* before the war which was very popular and continued to be put on even after 1968. Although his name as the translator was suppressed, he did receive a small royalty from these productions. 'I would walk past the theatre in the first snow of the season,' he said, 'shivering in my thin jacket, and see *Hamlet* announced as a coming attraction, and I would think, *good, I'll*

have an overcoat by Christmas!' That was how
they lived, in those days, he said, 'hand to mouth' –
whatever you say, say nothing – and then covered
his lips with his fingers and laughed, enjoying his
own wordplay. Zdeněk, for all his regrets – 'It was
too late for me,' he would cry, 'the Havel revolution, too late!' – is a great laugher. One day, when
we were in his car and I had been pressing him for
details of his life in 'those days', he began to
chuckle, and waved a hand at me, saying, 'Stop,
stop! You are like the ones who used to interrogate
me then, the nameless ones!' But then his smile
faded and he turned a grim face to the windscreen
again. What do I know?

The day was dying when we got back to the
hotel. The Professor left us, promising to pick us
up later and take us to his home. In the lobby the
two black-eyed beauties were at their post again
under the potted palm, fingering their coffee cups
and appraising the passing men, potential trade.
Such beautiful creatures, I wondered aloud as we
entered the lift, why did they take up such a
profession? 'I suppose,' J. said, 'they do it for
kecks.' We were too tired to laugh.

It is a peculiarly affecting, regressive sensation to
wake up from an involuntary sleep at evening in a
strange hotel room, the daylight all gone from the

window, and a lamp, an impassive sentinel, burning on the bedside table. The unfamiliar furniture
crouches in the shadows, looking as if it had been
engaged in a furtive passacaglia and had stopped
in its paces an instant before one opened one's
eyes. The noises from outside are different now,
more indistinct, it would seem, as if muffled by the
falling darkness. There is the hum of the great
concourse of office workers going home; voices
sound, and a radio buzzes somewhere, and car
tyres make a watery hissing in the dry streets.
One's day-clothes restrict, there is a hot dampness
in the crevices of elbows, behind the knees. Sluggishly one's mind casts about, fumbling like a
hand on the bed covers, trying to grasp something,
a fragment of thought, a dream, a memory, and
failing. What is it the moment is reminiscent of?
The silence, the hum in the air, the woolly warmth
. . . all this is out of the far, the immemorial, past.
Is it childhood that is nudging at the blunted edges
of consciousness, a jumbled recollection of the
fevered bedtimes of one's lost childhood? Somewhere adults are awake, going about their un-
sleeping, mysterious tasks.

How much of this first visit to Prague, twenty
years ago, am I remembering, and how much is
being invented for me? Memory is a vast, animated, time-ravaged mural. There is a fore-

ground, hazier in places than the extremest background, while in the middle distance the real business is going on, but so busily it is hard to make out. We fix on a face, a familiar room, a little scene; startlingly, off at the side, from nowhere, it might be, a pair of eyes look out at us directly from the crowd, fixing us with their candid glance, cool, amused, and quizzical, like the eyes of that mild maenad in Poussin's *Dance to the Music of Time*. There are, too, the big, continent-shaped patches of bare stucco, the damaged places that no restorer will mend, now. Some things of that first visit – and of other, more recent ones – I recall as vividly as if they were before me now, but they are almost all inconsequential. The hopeful money-changer in his leather jacket. The two prostitutes in the lobby, their lipstick, their hairstyles that long ago have gone out of fashion, even the imitation palm tree under which they sat. I see the Professor standing in the cathedral, pointing up earnestly at the stained-glass window. I see myself waking, fully dressed, on that big, high bed, not knowing where I was. Why these fragments and not others, far more significant? Why these?

The Professor's wife was short, dark, handsome and intense. Her name was, let us say, Marta.

The clothes she wore were too young for her, a tight black jumper and a black leather skirt, far too short, and black stockings. The outfit, at once severe – all that black – and slightly tartish, was I think a form of protest, a gesture of defiance against what she saw as the meanness and enforced conformity of her life. Of all the people I met in Prague that first time, no matter how oppressed or angry or despairing, she was the one who seemed to me truly a prisoner. There was a manic quality to her desperation, a sense of pent-up hysteria, as if she had passed the day, and so many other days, pacing the floor, from door to window, window to door, one hand plunged in her hair and the other clutching a shaking cigarette. She would have been frightening, in her violent discontent, had it not been for her humour. In the midst of a tirade against the State, against her family – she seemed to have a great many relatives, all of whom she professed to despise – she would suddenly stop and turn her face aside and give a snuffly cackle of laughter, and shake her head, and click her tongue, as if she had caught sight of a younger, happier, more cheerfully sceptical version of herself smiling at her and wagging a finger in rueful admonishment. I think that in her heart she simply could not credit her predicament, and lived in the angry conviction that a life so absurd and grotesque must be at any moment about to change. I liked her at once, the menacing black outfit, the scarlet fingernails, the frankly dyed hair, the flashing look that she gave me as, with a flamenco dancer's flourish of the shoulders, she handed me a bilious-green glass tumbler three-quarters full of vodka.

We were in a small, neat, bright room with a lot of blond, fake-Scandinavian furniture. Everywhere, on every available flat surface, Marta's collection of Bohemian glass vied for space with the Professor's books. Through an archway there was a galley kitchen where saucepans were seething and steaming. J. and G. and I sat crowded hip to hip on a narrow sofa, our knees pressed against the edge of a low coffee table. The Professor sat opposite us in what was obviously 'his' chair, an old wooden rocker draped with a faded, tasselled rug; when he grew animated, or when Marta was provoking him with one of her tirades, he would propel himself back and forth with steadily increasing speed until, just when it seemed the madly rearing chair would tip him forward on to the floor, he would grasp the armrests and pitch himself stiffly back against the headrest and go suddenly still, queasily smiling, like Dr Strangelove in his wheelchair, pinioned by a gravitational force all of his own. I made the first gaffe of the evening by asking how many rooms there were in the apartment. The Professor winced, and Marta in the galley turned from her steaming pots and gave a bitter snort of laughter; this room, it seemed, along with a tiny bathroom down the hall, was the extent of their living quarters. 'Our bed!' Marta said, pointing with a wooden spoon at the sofa where we were sitting. 'It unfolds,' the Professor corroborated helpfully, showing how with a graceful gesture of his hands. I am sure I was blushing.

While Marta was noisily busy at the stove, the Professor conducted us on an imaginary tour through the city's museums we had been unable to visit in reality. His modestly delivered disquisition on Czech art in the twentieth century was a revelation, to me, anyway. Most of the artists he mentioned were ones, I am ashamed to say, that I had never heard of. The extraordinary flowering of Modernism in Prague in the years just before and after the First World War was put into the shade by brasher capitals such as Paris and Vienna. The long-lived exile František Kupka, who settled permanently in Paris in 1895, was one of the great figures of European abstraction. He derived many of his ideas from music – he liked to describe himself as a 'colour symphonist'

– and photography, which he valued for its abstract possibilities. While Kupka was settling in Paris, the younger Prague painters were founding the Osma ('The Eight') group of avant-gardists, which in 1911 evolved into the Association of Plastic Arts, the cradle of Czech cubism. The greatest of the cubist artists was the sculptor Otto Gutfreund, although at the end of his career he abandoned the cube in favour of a kind of naïve realism. The most tangible mark that cubism left on the city was in architecture.[8] As early as 1911 the architect Josef Chochol was putting up some remarkable buildings below the hill of Vyšehrad. After the establishment of the Republic of Czechoslovakia at the end of hostilities in 1918 Prague became a sort of collection point for European avant-garde movements, particularly Surrealism, to which Praguers took with unsurprising enthusiasm. The city already had its own quasi-Dadaist movement, called Devětsil, of which Charlie Chaplin was granted honorary membership *in absentia*. Devětsil eventually imploded, but left a strong legacy in the Surrealist works of such artists as Josef Šíma and Jindřich Štyrský . . . Names, names. Listening to the

[8] Tangible indeed is the cubist lamppost in Jungmannovo náměstí, a fascinating but frankly hideous object designed by Vratislav Hofman in 1913.

Professor, I experienced a sense of shame such as a professional explorer would feel on being gently told that an entire civilisation had flourished briefly in the valley next to where he was born, the existence of which had been entirely unknown to him.

Over dinner, crowded together at a small square table wedged into a corner of the apartment, we attempted to move from art to a discussion of the frosty state of East–West relations. Marta, however, would have none of it. She wanted only to hear about America, land of freedom and limitless wealth. She complained that her son, although a diligent letter writer, never gave her the kind of details she desired. Were the department stores as magnificent as she had heard? Macy's, Bloomingdale's, I. Magnum, Nieman Marcus . . . each legendary name as she breathed it glowed like a coal. J. and G., disenchanted survivors of Berkeley 1968, tried to explain to her some of the realities of life in the Great Republic – there was much emphasis, I recall, on the plight of poor whites in the mining towns of Virginia – but she would have none of that, either, it was heresy to her ears. She was an educated woman, a chemist by training; she was not naïve, and certainly not uninformed; she listened to the Voice of America and the BBC World Service, when the signals were not jammed; she was well aware that the West had its pains and protests; but the fact was, she insisted, we could have no true idea of what it was like to live in one of the satellite countries of the Soviet empire. We continually spoke, she said, J. and G. and I, of Eastern Europe, she had listened to us doing so all evening – but could we not see that even by using that designation we were, however unwittingly, conniving with the Soviets and accepting the status quo? Eastern Europe? she said, glaring at each of us in turn – where was that? Where does Eastern Europe begin? At Moscow? Budapest? Prague? *Vienna?* The croissant, that quintessential staple of Parisian mornings, did we know the origin of it, that it took its shape from the crescent displayed on the flags of the Ottoman Empire that were carried to the very walls of Vienna before a terrified Europe at last mobilised itself sufficiently to push the forces of the infidel back to the East? No no, if there was an Eastern Europe, it began no further west than Istanbul!

Flushed by now, as were all of us, on bad Moravian wine, the Professor's wife had taken on a sort of furious magnificence, seemed a very Libuše – we shall meet Libuše presently – the raging mother of a country that at depressingly regular intervals throughout the twentieth century had been dishonoured, betrayed, invaded.[9] As she railed at us, the Professor watched her with brimming uxorious admiration, wordlessly urging her on. I have always been fascinated by the deals that married couples tacitly make with each other, the silent arrangements of inter-dependence by which they apportion power between them. Who could know how many times over the years the Professor himself had been dishonoured by the authorities, betrayed by friends and colleagues, had his privacy of heart and mind invaded, and how many times he had returned here, to this cramped sanctuary, exhausted in spirit, to feed and renew himself upon his wife's unrelenting fury, outrage and contempt in the face of State oppression? And now, having said her say, his wife retreated into silence, although her rage continued to make a palpable

[9] Milan Kundera, in his novel *Ignorance*, is awed by these repeating loops:

'The history of the Czechs in the twentieth century is graced with a remarkable mathematical beauty due to the triple repetition of the number twenty. In 1918, after several centuries, they achieved their independence and in 1938 they lost it.

'In 1948 the Communist revolution, imported from Moscow, inaugurated the country's second twenty-year span; that one ended in 1968 when, enraged by the country's insolent self-emancipation, the Russians invaded with half a million soldiers.

'The occupier took over in full force in the autumn of 1969 and then, to everyone's surprise, took off in autumn 1989 – quietly, politely, as did all the Communist regimes in Europe at that time: And that was the third twenty-year span.'

mutter and grumble, like the reverberations of a thunder storm that has departed to batten on some cowering elsewhere.

The Professor was considering his wine glass. Yes, he admitted mildly, all that Marta had said was true. There were intervals when life in Prague was almost unbearable, to him as much as to her. Curiously, perhaps, it was not the times of active oppression that were hardest – the aftermath of the communist takeover in May 1948, or of the Soviet invasion and annexation of the country twenty years later – for then at least there was a sense of dreadful excitement at the spectacle of something happening, even if what was happening was terrible. Afterwards, however, when authority was consolidated and the tanks were gone from the streets, an awful lethargy had quickly descended, and the country had slumped once more into a troubled but unshakeable somnolence. The Professor, still gazing at his glass, smiled ironically. He wished, he said, that he could blame this state of torpor on the Soviets, or even on home-grown petty tyrants, but the fact was, the Czechs had been sleepwalking for three and a half centuries, ever since, that is, the defeat at the Battle of White Mountain in 1620, when the Protestant forces of the young Frederick, Elector Palatine, appointed King of Bohemia

by the Prague Diet, and known ever afterwards
as the Winter King, were crushed by the Habsburg Emperor Frederick II, Jesuit-trained hammer of the Lutherans. Even the infatuated
Ripellino agrees with the Professor's gloomy
diagnosis, seeing the country as 'a land prostrate
and somnolent' since the disaster of White
Mountain. 'Prague,' he writes, 'has the rhythm
of slow, endless mastication (like that of Gregor
Samsa in *The Metamorphosis* for hours on end),
a catatonia from which it at times awakes with a
burst of energy that immediately dies down,' and
speaks of visitors being 'struck by the frailty of
the joyless, eternally pouting city, its suffocating,
defenceless lethargy, its deposed-sovereign majesty, the pallor, the morose resignation of those
who walk its constricted streets, a dungheap of
ancient glories.' The Professor, unlike Ripellino a
native son, after all, could not be as harsh in his
judgement as the jilted Italian, but even he, it was
obvious, had his days when he wished he could
take the city by the shoulders and shake it until its
stone monuments rattled in their sockets . . . And
yet, he said, he would not leave, could not leave,
not for all the gold paving of America's streets.

In the confused interregnum after August
1968, before the Soviets had fully taken over
and it was still comparatively easy to get out – in

the period more than a hundred thousand Czechs fled the country – Marta had begged him repeatedly that they should flee together to New York, to their son, who had a job there, and contacts at the university, and might even be able to find employment for the Professor. But the Professor would not budge – no, he would not budge. Marta was speaking again, as her husband continued to gaze dreamily into the dregs in his glass. 'You would quote those lines at me,' she accused him, 'those lousy lines in that lousy poem by that lousy poet Viktor Dyk, saying those who should dare to leave would die.[10] But you would not have died!' Yes, the Professor mildly agreed – it was apparent they had been through this conversation before, many times – he would have survived, but something in him would have died, for he would have lost an essential part of himself had he left Prague. He turned to us, his visitors. 'This,' he said, tapping a finger on the pale-pine table and making it for a moment Europe, 'this is civilisation, the only one I know.'

[10] The lines by Viktor Dyk are from the poem '*Země mluví*' (The Land Speaks), translated by Justin Quinn:

> *Opustíš-li mne, nezahynu.*
> *Opustíš-li mne, zahyneš!*
> *(If you leave me, I will not die.*
> *If you leave me, you will die!)*

After dinner Marta plied us with a sweet liqueur, a local speciality, the name of which I have forgotten – was it green, or was it just the glasses that were green? – and the Professor took from a drawer in his desk a music-case, exactly like, I saw with a start, the satchel that my sister had when we were children and she took piano lessons, an old leather one with a silver metal clasp like an attenuated dumbbell. He put the case on the coffee table and opened it flat. Inside was a sheaf of some thirty photographs, carefully wrapped in tissue paper. Perhaps it was the effect of the wine at dinner, and now the liqueur, but there seemed to me a vaguely religious, vaguely sacramental, tenor to the moment. And why not? True works of art are a real presence, after all.

The photographs were by Josef Sudek. They were in black-and-white, mostly views of Prague streetscapes, with a few interior studies, including 'Labyrinth in My Studio', two oneiric still-lifes from the 'Remembrances' series of the late 1960s, and the ravishing 'Nude', the one seated sideways with her hair partly hiding her face, from the early 1950s. I had not seen Sudek's work before; in fact, I had not heard of him before coming on this mission to Prague. He is, I believe, a great artist, in a league, or almost, with that other visual celebrant of a great city, the Parisian Eugène Atget, with whom he shares significant artistic traits. But these sober evaluations came later.

It is strange, that sense of familiarity one has on even a first encounter with an artist's work. As I looked at those photographs one by one I was convinced that I had seen them before, many times, and knew them well – that, indeed, there had never been a time when I did not already know them. Plato's by now trite notion must be true, that somewhere in the unconscious there is a myriad of ideal forms, the transcendent templates, as it were, against which is fitted and measured each new object that one encounters in the world. But there was a more immediate, less lofty, cause of the soft shock of recognition, a sort of shivery drizzle down the back of the mind, that I experienced as I took in these reticent yet ravishing, dreamy yet precise and always particular images. It was, simply, that in them I discovered Prague. Art, Henry James insisted in a famous letter of rebuke to the philistine H.G. Wells, art *makes* life, makes interest, makes importance', by which he may be understood to mean that the work of art singles out, 'beautifully', as H.J. himself would have it, the essential matters, the essential moments, in the disordered flux that is actual, lived life, while ever acknowledging the unconsidered but sustaining dross left behind, the Derridan *rien* that is supposedly *de hors-texte*. All day I had been walking about the city without seeing it, and suddenly now Sudek's photographs, even the private, interior studies, showed it to me, in all its stony, luminous solidity and peculiar, wan, absent-minded beauty. Here, with this sheaf of pictures on my knees, I had finally arrived.

Josef Sudek was born in the Bohemian town of Kolín in 1896 where in later years he would take some of his most evocative, Proustian pictures. His father died when he was three, and his mother moved the family to Prague. At fifteen he was apprenticed to a bookbinder in Nymburk, and later to one in Prague. At the outbreak of the First World War he was drafted into the army and sent to the Italian front, where a shell detonated by gunners from his own side damaged his right arm so badly that it had to be amputated. So ended his bookbinding career, before it had properly begun. When he was capable of being moved he was sent back to Prague and was lodged in the Veterans' Hospital to undergo a lengthy convalescence. He had already developed an interest in photography, and had taken his camera with him to the front and made numerous studies of his fellow soldiers and of the Italian countryside. In his lifetime he ventured abroad only once more, and that was to revisit Italy, and the scene of his wounding: 'Far outside the city toward dawn, in the fields bathed by the morning dew, I finally found the place. But my arm wasn't there . . .'

Faced now with the problem of finding work, Sudek spurned the government's offer that he should become a street vendor selling cigarettes and tobacco for the State monopoly. Instead, he tried to eke out his army pension by hawking photographs on the Prague boulevards. His time as a street seller did not last long, for he had no professional training as a photographer and could not secure the necessary tradesman's certificate. However, one of the staff at the Veterans' Hospital, Dr Nedoma – spiritual cousin, surely, to Van Gogh's Dr Gachet – had spotted Sudek's potential, and determination, and succeeded in having him enrolled in the photography class of the Prague School of Graphic Arts. Despite the disapproval of his conservative professor, Karel Novák – 'a noble gentleman,' as Sudek would later wryly describe him – he got through the course, and received a certificate establishing him as a professional photographer in 1924. Thereafter, his work came to the attention of a publishing house, Družstevní Práce (Co-operative Work), which began to give him freelance commissions, enabling him to move into a little studio – hardly more than a garden shed, really – on Újezd, between Malá Strana and the river, which was to be both his workplace and his home for the next thirty years of his life.

The studio was already equipped with photographic equipment, most of it antique pieces from the previous century, which Sudek found perfectly congenial; after all, he was himself a relic of the nineteenth century, if not an earlier era. In the late 1940s he found a camera, a Kodak panoramic, dating from 1894, which might have been made to his specifications, although it had only two shutter speeds. It was a big, awkward brute, but it was his brute, and he loved it, not least for the fact that it was two years older than he was. That even with only one arm he managed to haul it about the city and the countryside is a matter of some amazement, but haul it he did, taking some of his finest pictures, including the series 'Vanished Statues', 1952–1970, stark, austerely beautiful studies of crippled trees that he chanced upon in his rambling through the forests near where he was born. It is perhaps too obvious, given Sudek's poised reticence as an artist, to see in the many images he fixed of these maimed giants a composite, covert self-portrait.

By the early 1950s he had mastered the technical difficulties of the panoramic camera. A problem that initially frustrated him was that the camera could take only one 10×30 cm strip of film at a time, and when it had been exposed he was forced to return to the darkroom to put in a new one. Božena Rothmayerová, a textile artist and wife of Sudek's friend, the architect Otto Rothmayer, solved the problem for him by making a black sack that was large enough to accommodate man and camera; when he had taken his picture, he would kneel down on the spot, whether alone in the woods or among the crowds on a city street, crawl with his camera into the lightless sack and, working by touch, insert the new film. It is a pity there is no photograph of Sudek in his sack: it would be an apposite image of an artist whom some critics claim for the Surrealist camp, although his supposedly surreal photographs are surely too plainly playful and witty to be thus labelled.

It was the Kodak that made possible one of his finest achievements, the volume *Panoramic Prague*, published in 1959. His other great portfolio, and his first published work, is the one he made of St Vitus's Cathedral, commissioned by the publishers Družstevní Práce, which appeared in 1928 to mark the – supposed – completion of

reconstruction work on the building. The portfolio consisted of sixty sets of fifteen prints, all of
them processed by Sudek himself. These photographs are among Sudek's most weighty archi-
tectural studies, surpassed only by the 'Contrasts'
series of 1942, when he returned to photographing the cathedral, where, as we can see from his
recording of it, renovation work was still in
progress. By now he had adopted the difficult
but immensely rewarding technique of contact
printing, that is, making photographs direct from
negatives to paper in the darkroom, with no
possibility of correction. In 1940 he had chanced
upon a large contact print of a statue in Chartres
Cathedral taken at the turn of the century, and
immediately recognised the possibilities of this
way of working. Contact printing yielded effects
that the method of enlarging could not – 'From
that day onward,' he later said, 'I never made
another enlargement.' In the pre-Kodak days,
this change of work practice meant using large
glass negatives, some of them up to 40×50 cm.
The technique was both painstaking and time-
consuming, and Sudek made very few prints from
each negative – which, incidentally, is why the
photographs the Professor wanted us to take to
his son were so valuable.

A wonderful account of Sudek at work is

provided by his champion and chronicler, Zdeněk Kirschner, of Prague's Museum of Decorative Arts:

> When Sudek placed his heavy wooden view camera on his sturdy tripod, unwrapped his lenses from their pieces of cloth, selected the right one, inserted it in the camera, crept under the black cloth he called 'a nun', considered the composition and observed the light, adjusted the equipment, slid in the photographic plate and opened the aperture mechanically or by uncovering the small 'hat' from the lens, then as the light began to paint the picture on the negative, and only then, would he pronounce his magic sentence, '*A hudba hraje . . .*' 'And the music plays . . .'

Another celebratory witness is the photographer Sonja Bullaty, a survivor of the concentration camps who worked with him after the war – his 'apprentice-martyr', he called her – and who would mount a one-man show of his photographs at her gallery in New York in 1971. Observing that 'the whole of Sudek's life seemed to revolve around light', she goes on:

> I remember one time, in one of the Romanesque halls, deep below the spires of the cathedral – it was

as dark as in the catacombs – with just a small window below street level inside the massive medieval walls. We set up the tripod and camera and then sat down on the floor and talked. Suddenly Sudek was up like lightning. A ray of sun had entered the darkness and both of us were waving cloths to raise mountains of ancient dust 'to see the light,' as Sudek said. Obviously he had known that the sun would reach here perhaps two or three times a year and he was waiting for it.

She also recalls accompanying him to the city's old cemeteries, where Sudek took some of his most affecting and intensely felt pictures:

I liked the early evenings when a mysterious sadness crept in and Sudek sat waiting for the last rays of the sun on an old gravestone. It was more familiar here for me, for during the Nazi occupation cemeteries were the only green spaces allowed to those wearing the Jewish star.

Although Sudek is a great landscape artist, Prague was his prime subject. Vladimir Nabokov, speaking of *Lolita*, remarked on the task that he set himself in that novel of 'inventing' America. Readers may find this a startling claim, and an arrogant one, but this is only what all artists do, they *invent reality*; for that is the nature of art, that, in James's ringing affirmation, it *'makes* life, makes interest, makes importance'. In the early days of Nazi occupation, when to be caught photographing anything that might be deemed sensitive, even landscapes, could lead to the gallows, Sudek virtually retreated into his studio; instead of restriction, what he found there was a kind of interior freedom. This was when he embarked on the two superb series, 'The Window of My Studio' (1940–1954) and 'A Walk in My Garden' (1940–1976). The window pictures in particular, many of them shot through misted-over panes, are masterly, at once mysterious and homely, evocative and enigmatic. And although these pictures might have been taken anywhere, they are somehow quintessential of Prague.

Sudek was a kind of alchemist in this city of alchemists. Those who knew him recall with awe the magical atmosphere of the darkroom in his studio, where even in summer the air felt chilled, Zdeněk Kirschner notes, and 'where holes had been worn into the floor over the years, and rows of wood shelves overflowed with glass jars of chemicals. Sudek mixed all of his own developing solutions and fixatives himself for the photographs he alone printed. Stories abound about the mysteries of his darkroom, and his reliance on experience and instinct more than prescribed measurements in his work. Each print he produced is unique and cannot be duplicated.' The studio itself, crammed to the ceilings with papers, prints, pictures, books, clocks, candles, gramophone records, all sorts of precious objects – memorabilia, junk, the detritus of a lifetime – inevitably conjures up the wonder-rooms of the fortress of Hradčany where the obsessive Rudolf II stored his haphazard collection of treasures and trash, a vast jumbled barricade erected vainly against the encroaching death that he so feared. Indeed, there is one picture in the 'Labyrinths' series, taken in 1969, of a teetering mass of paper-rolls seen end-on, which might have been assembled by Arcimboldo himself, Rudolf's court painter, that *ingegnosissimo pittor fantastico* and Surrealist *avant la lettre* who built his picture-portraits out of random objects piled together into grotesque jigsaw puzzles.

The Czechoslovak state conferred a number of bombastic-sounding honours on Sudek – he was given the title 'Artist of Merit' in 1961 and awarded the 'Order of Work' in 1966 – but he had his critics within the system, who charged him with being aloof from common life, and accused him of being a romantic, an accusation to which he happily pleaded guilty. There were grumbles too that he concentrated overmuch on nature, and included too few people in his pictures[11]; he retorted that it took him so much time to set up his equipment that by the time he was ready to shoot, everyone around had disappeared. It is remarkable that work so delicate and sensuous, so luminous, could have been produced in such dark times. Sudek lived through two wars, the first of which he very nearly did not survive; at one end of his life he witnessed the collapse of the Austro-Hungarian Empire in 1918, at the other he experienced the Soviet invasion of 1968; in between, there was the 1948 communist takeover and the fall of a forty-year night. Yet even out of darkness he could make work that glowed – his nocturnal studies of Prague are among his finest achievements. He was a romantic in the best sense, in that through impeccable technique his work speaks directly to the spirit. All who knew him testify to his genuine simplicity, his diffidence, his sense of humour. He was a poor boy from the provinces, not well educated, as he admitted. The war damaged him, took his arm and left him with who knows what inner torments. He was not polished,

[11] In a conversation in Paris recently with Henri Cartier-Bresson and his wife, the photographer Martine Franck, I was told they found Sudek's work 'not human enough'.

he was not an intellectual. When he entered the Prague School of Graphic Arts, he told Sonja Bullaty, 'Professor Karel Novák was a noble gentleman, intelligent, you could tell right away, because he withstood my cursing and statements the way they stayed in my vocabulary from the war.' Yet he was not brutalised. After photography his greatest love was music – the Professor and Marta had warm memories of Sudek's Tuesday night 'concerts', when he would receive friends at his studio and play records for them on his homemade turntable – and he had a close affinity with the work of Janáček, whose birthplace, Hukvaldy, was the subject of his last book. Indeed, Janáček's is perhaps the art that his own most resembles, in its intensity and sense of yearning, its stark dynamics, its precise feeling for a homeland. Sudek's aesthetic was simple, and can be summed up in this statement from him, recorded by Bullaty: 'Discovery – that's important. First comes the discovery. Then follows the work. And then sometimes something remains from it.' Prague has more famous sons, but none of them, not even Kafka, managed to capture so movingly the essence of the place, its mystery and weary charm, its tragic beauty, its light and shadow, and that something in between, the peculiar, veiled radiance of this city on the Vltava.

When I think back to those days, and nights, in Prague, I am not sure whether what I am summoning up are images from my memory, or from the photographs of Josef Sudek, so thoroughly has his work become for me an emblem of the place. I try to recall our leavetaking of the Professor and his wife; they lived in an anonymous apartment block on an unremarkable street to the west of Wenceslas Square, yet what I see is a scene straight out of one of Sudek's nocturnes, something like the view of Prašný Bridge on a snowy evening, or that lamp-lit cobbled square on Kampa Island, with the winter tree, and the Charles Bridge behind, and the city farther off, the light of the street lamp in the foreground all blurred and gauzy, as if seen through tears. At the door, Marta clutched G.'s hand in hers and bade her 'Say hello for me to California,' a greeting that sounded to our ears more like a farewell to an impossible dream. I do not think that Marta made it to America, in the end, although it is not impossible that she did. A couple of years ago we heard that the Professor had died. How quickly the past becomes the past! That night we walked in silence, the three of us, though the empty, frostbound streets back to our hotel. G. carried the photographs, rolled up tightly and concealed in a cardboard tube supposedly containing nothing more than a reproduction of a poster from the 1930s for an exhibition of formalist Czech art. Next morning, under a shower of sleet, we left the city by train. At the Austrian border we were held up for an hour while crossing guards went through the carriages with implements like giant versions of dentist's mirrors, searching under the seats and on the luggage racks for anyone who might have hidden there in an attempt to flee the country. My palms were damp: what if G. were to be made to open the cardboard tube and show its contents? But the guards were not interested in art. When we crossed to the Austrian side the first thing I saw was a hoarding of a half-naked woman advertising some degenerate Western luxury – Dior fashions or Mercedes motor cars – and something in me revelled instinctively, irresistibly, in the sight of what seemed such happy, hopeful, life-affirming colours, and I thought of the Professor, and Marta, and felt ashamed.

2

THRESHOLD

My brief history of the Czech Lands, down-loaded from the Internet, opens by observing that the first inhabitants of the region were pre-historic fish. The anonymous author of this dis-concertingly skittish document – why do I think it was written by a woman? – goes on to note that when the prehistoric oceans dried up, the fish were followed by dinosaurs, mammoths, and, in due course, Celts. The Celts, that mysterious but ubiquitous people, which some specialists claim never existed, arrived in the fourth century BC; the Roman name for the area, Boiohaemum, our Bohemia, is said to have derived from the Boii, one of the Celtic tribes. Presently this race of redheads was displaced by Germanic tribes from the west, and by Romans from the south, although the latter did not progress much beyond the Danube. Some centuries of apparent inactivity followed, for historians are largely silent on the period until the sixth century of our era, when the Slavs arrived, and occupied the left bank of the Vltava, above what is now Vyšehrad. Here, by the end of the ninth century, a citadel was established by the first of the Přemyslids, one Bořivoj; this was the original seat of the Přemysl dynasty and not, so the sometimes censorious *Blue Guide* scoffingly asserts, the fortress at Vyšehrad, 'as legend would have us believe'. In the meantime, Italian, French, German and Jewish merchants had been setting themselves up on the opposite bank, in the area that is now Nové Město, or New Town; it was connected to the Slavic quarter by a wooden bridge, and must have been a lively spot. In the later 960s the city was visited by Ibrahim ibn Ya'qub, a Spanish Jew dispatched from Cordoba by Caliph al-Hakam II as part of a diplomatic mission to the Emperor Otto I in Merseburg. The bookish but well-travelled Ibrahim, who would have known a thing or two about the cities of the earth, was impressed by Prague's moneyed cosmopolitanism.

Legend, as the *Blue Guide* knows, has a deplorably lurid imagination, and in the matter of Prague's origins will have none of that boring stuff about Migrations of the Peoples and dynast's first seats. No no, listen, it says excitedly in its rough demotic, this is how it was: once upon a time in the east there were these three brothers, Czech, Lech and Rus. Seeking new homelands, they set out westward at the head of their respective tribes. Rus halted at the Dnieper and became Father Russia, while the other two continued on, Lech veering northwards to found Poland, and Czech climbing Říp hill in Bohemia and deciding that he liked all that he saw. Czech's tribe settled down happily here, and after a couple of hundred years produced a new leader rejoicing in the name of Krok[12] who lived at legendary Vyšehrad. Krok had three beautiful daughters, Kazi the healer, Teta the priestess, and Lady Libuše the prophetess. Presently Libuše inherited her father's throne and became ruler of the Czech Lands. However, since Czech's male descendants, like most men, then as now, did not relish the idea of living in a matriarchy – or, as my Internet history Runyonesquely puts it, 'a guy who did not like one of Libuše's decisions as judge started a stink about the fact that the Czechs were ruled by a woman' – Libuše followed the dictates of a vision and sent a company of her subjects, accompanied by her white horse,

---

[12] And we wonder at the bizarre nomenclature of Kafka's characters!

into the forest in search of an *oráč*, a ploughman, building a *práh*, a threshold of a house, and there to found a *nové město*, a 'new town'. People and horse carried Přemysl Oráč – Oráč the Ploughman – in triumph back to Vyšehrad Castle on its stony eminence above the Vltava, where he and Libuše were married, thus founding the Přemyslid dynasty . . .

How curious it is, the way in which one's fancy lingers on the least of history's props, and how, lingered on, the props spring suddenly to life. Beyond all this welter of names and dates and places, my attention keeps wandering back to that wooden bridge over the Vltava that linked the New Town on the right bank to the old Slav quarter on the left. What did it look like, how was it built? No sooner have the questions formed than the mind begins to drive the piles into the mud and link the arches one by one. Romantically, legendarily, I see it in storm, straining against the surge of waters, or hovering on the mist of mornings, or glimmering in the darkness of the vast medieval night . . . In the eleventh century the wooden structure was replaced by a stone one, 'the so-called Judith's Bridge' of the *Blue Guide* – but why 'so-called'? – and in time that too was replaced, when the great architect Peter Parléř, summoned to Prague in the city's Golden Age by the Holy Roman Emperor Charles IV, in 1357 built the bridge named after the Emperor that stands to this day, despite fire and flood and the generations of war.

At least, I think it was Peter Parléř who built it . . .

In the essay *Building Dwelling Thinking*, the philosopher Martin Heidegger meditates movingly on the essential nature of the bridge, the bridge's *bridgeness*, as *der Meister aus Deutschland* himself might put it. The bridge defines, brings into existence. 'It does not just connect banks that are already there. The banks emerge as banks only as the bridge crosses the stream . . . It brings stream and bank and land into each other's neighbourhood. The bridge *gathers* the earth as landscape around the stream.' The bridge is a 'location,' he writes, 'it allows a space into which earth and heaven, divinities and mortals are admitted.' Heidegger designates the bridge as a 'thing', in the ancient sense of gathering or assembly. 'The bridge is a thing and *only that*. Only? As this thing it gathers the fourfold.'

Always and ever differently the bridge escorts the lingering and hastening ways of men to and fro, so that they may get to other banks and in the end, as mortals, to the other side. Now in a high arch, now

in a low, the bridge vaults over glen and stream –
whether mortals keep in mind this vaulting of the
bridge's course or forget that they, always themselves on their way to the last bridge, are actually
striving to surmount all that is common and un-
sound in them in order to bring themselves before
the haleness of the divinities. The bridge *gathers*, as
a passage that crosses, before the divinities –
whether we explicitly think of, and visibly *give
thanks for*, their presence, as in the figure of the
saint of the bridge, or whether that divine presence
is obstructed or even pushed wholly aside.

The bridge *gathers* to itself in *its own* way earth
and sky, divinities and mortals.

To stand on the Charles Bridge today, among the
press of tourists and moody sightseers – the sights
are always so much less than it seemed they
would be – is to feel the essential truth of Heidegger's numinous definitions, however unnumi-
nous may be the present-day reality of Prague,
heritage city of heritage cities.

River, bridge, the human community . . .

Vyšehrad Castle on its crag was the seat of the
Přemyslid rulers for a half century from 1085,
when King Vratislav I settled his court there.
After 1140, when the Přemyslids moved back
to Prague Castle on the left bank of the river,

Vyšehrad ceased to be a centre of royal power until Charles IV turned his omnivorous attention to the area and rebuilt the castle and erected fortifications, the mighty remains of which are still to be seen. During the Hussite wars of the fifteenth century most of Charles's handiwork was destroyed. Subsequently, Vyšehrad became a small independent town of traders and craftsmen, which in turn was flattened by the steamroller of history to make way for yet another fortress. The effects of these successive declines and falls are palpable still in the sombre, silvery air that seems so much thinner on those heights than down in the Old Town or even in melancholy Malá Strana. Vyšehrad lures few tourists, a fact that adds immeasurably to its charm. It is best approached from the metro station, despite the looming Palace of Culture, a typical example of brutalist gigantism from the communist era, and the equally awful Corinthia Towers Hotel which, by a piece of glum serendipity, finds itself overlooking a prison – the exercise yard had to be roofed over to spare the hotel's guests the sight of the prisoners at break time plodding their doleful circles. Leaving these horrors behind, one enters Na Bučance, another of Prague's inexplicably deserted and faintly sinister streets. Here is the Tábor Gate, there the Church of SS Peter and

Paul. The Rotunda of St Martin is a Romanesque jewel, still functioning as a church, one of the tiniest I have ever entered. The cemetery boasts the graves of, among many others, the composers Dvořák and Smetana – the latter wrote an opera based on the legend of Libuše and her lusty ploughman – and the writers Karel Čapek and Jan Neruda. Walk on and you enter a lonely little park – the Czech word for garden, *sad*, seems, for the English-speaker, peculiarly appropriate here – incongruously peopled by four sets of enormous stone figures by Josef Myslbek, another occupant of the nearby cemetery, representing not only, and inevitably, Libuše and Přemysl, but also Záboj and Slavoj, the latter described by my *Eyewitness Travel Guide* as 'mythical figures invented by a forger of old legends'. The statues were moved here in 1945 from their original site, the Palacký Bridge, damaged by American bombs in February that year. That is another characteristic of bridges, unremarked in Heidegger's dithyramb: they tend, unhappily, to attract bombardment.

What do I recall most clearly from my last visit to Vyšehrad? I draw up an inventory. Dead, damp leaves beside a gravel pathway. A mother and her toddler wandering through the cemetery in a vaguely questing way, as if these were not graves on either side but supermarket shelves. A nun in the Rotunda of St Martin, lighting a candle and smiling blissfully, angelically, to herself. Black spires seen through the bare black limbs of a winter tree. That soft-spoken man in a blue jersey sitting at a small square table selling entrance tickets to SS Peter and Paul's – of the church itself I retain practically nothing . . . Thinking historically, like giving a story a happy ending, is a matter of deciding where to stop. Hegel at Jena, writing on the Absolute, hears under his window Napoleon and his forces riding to battle and conceives of the little Corsican as the embodiment of the World Spirit. Napoleon, meanwhile, is pondering his haemorrhoids, those same haemorrhoids that may well have been one of the chief causes of his defeat at Waterloo. Everything ramifies. Facts are susceptible to an infinite process of dismantlement. Benoit Mandelbrot, the originator of fractal geometry, considered the question of how long, exactly, is a coastline? That is, at what level may we stop measuring the coast of Europe, say, and proclaim definitively that it is so many hundreds of thousands of miles long? If we employ a yardstick, the figure will be very much smaller than if we measure by the inch. Think of all those bays, those coves, those inlets; those dunes, those rocks, those grains of clay; those atoms, those electrons, those nuclei; those quarks, those super-strings . . . think, and immediately you plunge headlong into the dizzying possibility of there being no level at which to stop. So it is with the past. Is history the big picture, or the minute details, the grand sweep or the dusty annals? Irish historians are engaged in a passionate debate between revisionists and traditionalists. Revisionists want a new interpretation of ancient pieties – perhaps, they suggest, the famines of the 1840s were not entirely the fault of Perfidious Albion, perhaps the 1916 Rising was not the glorious blood sacrifice we have always been told that it was – while the traditionalists, many of whom see historiography as a tool for nation building, insist on a kind of poeticised, nationalist version of our shared past. In the Vyšehrad Cemetery there is a special section, the Slavín, or Pantheon, built by the architect Wiehl in the early 1890s, overlooked by stylised statues of the 'Rejoicing Homeland' and the 'Mourning Homeland', and containing the remains of some fifty of the home-land's heroes, including the Art Nouveau painter Alfons Mucha and the musician Jan Kubelík. In monuments such as the Slavín we encounter a notion of the past far removed from that of the young Anthony Burgess's schoolboy friend who encouraged him to read the history plays of Shakespeare since they were all to do with 'fighting and fucking tarts'.

The question I am addressing is the one that historian, tourist and essayist alike must grapple with: how and where to locate the 'real' Prague, if, indeed, such a singular thing may be said to exist. Those dead leaves that I remember beside the path on the heights of Vyšehrad, what is there about them that makes them particular to the place? When I think of Golden Lane I see far more vividly the snow under my feet, compacted to clouded grey glass, the first time I walked there with the Professor, than I do the house where in the late autumn and winter of 1916 Kafka wrote the stories that would make up the collection *A Country Doctor*. The gloomy glories of St Vitus's Cathedral are no more than a shimmer at the edge of my memory compared to the uncanny clarity with which I recall one afternoon leaving the crowded building, with its gaggles of tourists following the upheld umbrellas and rolled newspapers of their tour guides, and walking down the unexpectedly deserted Jiřská Street and hearing my own footsteps ring on the cobbles with what seemed definite but inexplicable intent. I met no one in particular, saw nothing out of the ordinary, so why has the image of myself walking there lodged so stubbornly in my recollection? Was it that the fresh-cut white stone paving flags and bags of mortar stacked against the east wall of the cathedral reminded me of Sudek's great series of photographs of St Vitus's under reconstruction in the 1920s? I do not know, just as I cannot say for certain what is the true length of the coastline of Europe. All I know is that I can see myself there, can see the silver-and-pearl light of afternoon, the gleam on the cobbles, that Japanese man frowning at his map, a grubby dog trotting past on its way to something important. These are the things we remember. It is as if we were to focus our cameras on the great sights and the snaps when developed all came out with nothing in them save undistinguished but maniacally detailed foregrounds.

If Prague is not place, is it people, then? Not the great sights but the great figures? The Emperor Charles IV (1316–78) in 1355 made Prague the capital of the Holy Roman Empire, the 'Rome of the North', thus initiating the city's Golden Age, attracting artists and scholars from all over Europe, including the poet Petrarch. Charles, son of John of Luxembourg, the blind soldier who died at the Battle of Crécy – a *blind soldier?* – was elected King of Germany in 1347 and crowned Holy Roman Emperor in 1355. He proceeded to shift power away from Italy and the papacy, and built his empire on the core of Bohemia and Moravia. His 'Golden Bull' of 1356 formed a new constitution for the empire, set out the procedures for imperial elections and the rights of the seven electors, declaring their domains indivisible. Prague expanded under Charles's rule; the horse and cattle markets, today's Wenceslas and Charles Squares, were incorporated into the New Town, work began on St Vitus's Cathedral, and the first university in central Europe was instituted. Charles was an extraordinarily liberal and enlightened ruler, highly intelligent and richly cultured, a vivid historical mover and achiever. Yet I cannot see him. The image I have of him is of one of those statues that are carried aloft in religious processions, gilded and impassive and mechanically nodding. Far more real to me is his blind old dad, lover of jousts and military adventuring, last seen hacking sightlessly all round him with his great-sword on the field at Crécy.

The single historical figure who most epitomises old Prague is the Emperor Rudolf II. This melancholy madman, gull of all manner of mountebanks and charlatans but also a patient patron of the astronomers Tycho Brahe and Johannes Kepler, was born in 1552 into one of the more complicated Habsburg lines. His father, the Holy Roman Emperor Maximilian II, son of the Emperor Ferdinand I and Emperor Charles V's brother, married Charles's daughter Maria. All right, all right, let us put it another way. Rudolf's father was Emperor Maximilian II. Maximilian was the son of Emperor Ferdinand I, who was brother to Emperor Charles V, founder of the Habsburg dynasty – the daddy of them all, as one might say. Maximilian married his cousin Maria, daughter of Charles V. As the attentive reader will already have spotted, this of course meant that Rudolf was by double lineage the great-grandson of Joanna the Mad![13] No wonder there were blemishes in Rudolf's psychological profile. Still, what family does not have its own version of Mad Joanna, squawking and jumping up and down on her perch somewhere amid the denser foliage of the family tree?

At the age of eleven, on the insistence of his mother, the mournful Maria, Rudolf was packed off from the relative liberality of his father Maximilian's court at Vienna to live in the household of the Spanish King Philip II, his mother's broth-

[13] Joanna was Queen of Castile and Léon, wife of Philip I of Spain, and mother of Charles V. After the death of her husband, poor Joanna lost her mind, and apart from a brief period of joint rule with Charles, spent the rest of her life shut up in the castle of Tordesillas. Ah, those crowned heads of Europe . . .

er, there to be taught some of the harsher realities of life as a Catholic monarch in a Europe facing into the horrors of the Counter-Reformation. During the seven years he spent in Madrid, Rudolf became, in Ripellino's wòrds, 'a perfect "Spaniard", acquiring the customs and masks of that dissembling monarchy. Bigotry, intrigues, religious pomp, suspicion, persecution of heretics, the Inquisition's funeral pyres, the illusion of boundless majesty, vainglory on land and at sea – such was his school.' This was a disastrous experience for the dreamy and otherworldly Rudolf, who was more interested in alchemy, literature, and the wilder shores of art – it was Rudolf who brought Arcimboldo, that master of the grotesque, to Prague and made him one of his chief court painters – than in power and the machinations of European politics. Ripellino is firm in his conviction that the Spanish experience was a 'fatal influence' on the young man's character: 'it heightened his morbid shyness, his yearning for solitude, and planted the seeds for the megalomania and persecution complex that later so obsessed him.' Spanish influence became very powerful at Rudolf's court, as the Jesuit-educated younger generation displaced the older, liberal Catholic faction. The new men, supported by Rome and Madrid, were the ones who prosecuted fiercely the Counter-Reformation measures that would lead, after Rudolf's time, to the Thirty Years War. So strong was the Spanish presence that in Bohemia the more fervent Catholics were known as *španělé*, 'Spaniards'.

Jealous, paranoid, hypochondriacal, incurably melancholy, obsessed with the passage of time and terrified at the prospect of death, Rudolf was a compulsive collector, filling room after room of Prague Castle with talismanic objects meant to stave off mortality and be a barrier against the world, all sorts of rubbish and kitsch tumbling together with exquisite *objets d'art*. As is so often the case with weak men who inherit vast power, he was obsessed with things in miniature, hiring entire schools of craftsmen to carve and emboss and inlay the tiniest surfaces, of pearls, nut shells, cherry pits, flakes of amber, birds' eggs, sharks' teeth, gallstones. No expense was spared, no effort was thought too great. He purchased a painting in Venice, *Das Rosenkranzfest*, by one of his favourite artists, Albrecht Dürer, and had it carried on foot across the Alps by four stout men, one at each corner.

Ripellino fairly revels in Rudolf's collectomania: 'Among the many peculiar objects he collected I might mention . . . an iron chair

(*Fangstuhl*) that held whoever sat in it a prisoner; a musical clock with a gilt lid decorated by a hunting scene of leaping stags; an *Orgelwerk* that performed "ricercars, madrigals, and canzoni" by itself; stuffed ostriches; rhinoceros chalices for boiling poisonous potions; a votive medallion of Jerusalem clay; the lump of soil from the Hebron Valley out of which Yahweh Elohim formed Adam; the large mandrake roots (alrauns) in the shape of little men reclining on soft velvet cushions in small cases resembling doll beds . . . [which] belong to the same family of man-like figures as the Golem, robots and Kafka's *odradek*.' But that is only the merest sample. Ripellino goes on to compile an 'unsystematic inventory' to represent the crowding and chaos in Rudolf's wonder-rooms:

Plaster casts of lizards and reproductions of other animals in silver, *Meermuscheln*, turtle shells, nacres, coconuts, statuettes of coloured wax, figurines of Egyptian clay, elegant mirrors of glass and steel, spectacles, corals, 'Indian' boxes filled with gaudy plumes, 'Indian' containers of straw and wood, 'Indian', that is, Japanese paintings, burnished silver and gilt 'Indian' nuts and other exotic objects the great carracks brought from India under full sail, a skin-coloured plaster-covered female torso of the kind the Prague Surrealists so loved, amber and ivory boards for playing dice, a skull of yellow amber, amber goblets, bagpipes, 'landscapes' of Bohemian jasper, a small table of enamelled silver, shells of agate, jasper, topaz and crystal, a silver picture in an ebony frame, a bas-relief in oriental alabaster, painted stones, mosaics, a small silver altar, a crystal goblet with a silver lid, a topaz carafe given to Rudolf by a Muscovite delegation, a carafe of 'starstone', a glass jug of Bohemian agate with a gold handle, a large topaz drinking vessel in the shape of a lion, ruby-inlaid gold tableware, clay pitchers (some of which are covered with red velvet), a coral ship with figurines, a ship of gilt wood, a tiny ship of silver-plated Cocus de Malediva, a jewel casket of rock crystal, a casket of mother of pearl, a silver lute, lamina of lapis lazuli, rhinoceros horns, ivory hunting horns, gaudy knives inlaid with gold and gems, porcelain, scraps of silk, globes of various guise including a silver one atop a hypogryph, armillary spheres, measuring instruments, Venetian glassware, an ancient head of Polyphemus, Deianeira and the centaur in silver, medals, maiolica in many colours, anatomical specimens, harnesses, spurs, bridles, rough wooden saddles, domed pavilions, doublets and other booty left by the Turks during their mounted forays, hunting gear, banners, muzzles and collars, every kind of plate, ostrich-egg goblets, sabres, cut-throat daggers, muskets, stilettos, sword cases, mortar pieces, pistols and verdugas. And automata and musical clocks. Clocks, clocks and more clocks.

Mopping our brow, we take a step back from the glare of Ripellino's coruscating romanticism and consult a cooler source. In his authoritative study of Rudolf, the historian R.J.W. Evans identifies three distinct versions of the Emperor which have come down to us. First there is the 'feeble, unstable and impoverished monarch' whose reign began in glory but ended with him humiliatingly deposed by his brother Matthias and cowering in terror within the fastness of Hradčany; second, the great connoisseur and patron of the arts and sciences; and third, the 'wizard Emperor' in thrall to magicians such as John Dee and Edward Kelley, an adept of astrology, Hermeticism, the Cabala, 'and plain old-fashioned superstition'. While not wholly dismissing any of these versions – a man may be a multitude, after all – Evans sets out to show not only how they overlap one upon the other, but that beneath the multifariousness of Rudolf's character there was an underlying unity. 'However hazardous it may be to speak of the philosophy of an age, there was nevertheless an underlying atmosphere, a climate of thought in later sixteenth-century Europe, which was particularly characteristic of the Imperial court in Prague . . . Part of the evidence for this is the universalist striving itself, an effort to preserve the mental and political unity of Christendom, to avoid religious schism, uphold peace at home, and deliver Europe from the Ottoman menace.' Even Rudolf's dabblings in magic may be viewed not as a vulgar delving after dark powers but part of a great stirring of intellectual curiosity and adventurousness which led directly to the Enlightenment.[14] Even John Dee, for so long viewed as a fraudulent opportunist and *Quacksalb*, has been radically reassessed, notably by the Renaissance scholar Frances Yates. Certainly Dee was an alchemist and necromancer, but he was also a geographer and mathematician, a bibliophile, a teacher of Sir Philip Sidney, and published books on mathematics, navigation, and the calendar.

'The occult striving,' Evans writes, 'was in essence an attempt to penetrate beyond the world

---

[14] In this regard it is instructive to recall that the great rationalist mathematician Sir Isaac Newton devoted much of his later life to alchemical studies, not to mention biblical exegesis and, in his position as controller of the Royal Mint, hunting down forgers and seeing them hanged.

of experience to the reality which underlay it, and as such it paralleled or overlapped with the artistic use of symbol and emblem. At the same time it belonged in a central way to the whole apprehension of nature during Rudolf's age, for the natural philosophers of the period were men who studied the forces at work in the world around them, not as discretely observed patterns of cause and effect, but as motive spirits acting through a divine scheme of correspondences.' Thus it is possible to regard Rudolf's band of alchemists in their laboratories in Vikářská lane not as black magicians but as something like today's quantum physicists, probing the mysterious and contradictory reality of the world. Like the alchemists before them, modern physicists work in far deeper darkness than the layman realises, trusting their instincts and making judgements as often on aesthetic as on purely 'scientific' grounds. Evans: 'The object of such a philosophy [alchemy] was not only to describe the hidden forces of nature but also to control them, since the initiate who understood their powers could also apply his knowledge.' At the outset Evans points out that Rudolf held to the traditional, earth-centred cosmology, and 'the notions to which he and so many of his contemporaries subscribed were in their very essence magical. They believed that the world of men and the world of nature were linked by hidden sources of knowledge, and that the problems of alchemy, astrology, or the Hermetic texts were proper subjects for learned investigation.' Against this, more than one of Rudolf's contemporaries insisted that there was nothing high-minded about his obsession with magic, and that all he wanted from his alchemists was that they should discover how to transmute base metal into gold so that he might replenish the imperial coffers that his crazed collecting was constantly threatening to empty.

The overseer of Rudolf's collections was the Italian antiquary Jacopo Strada, a resourceful and cunning scholar who not only amassed a huge treasury of coins, medallions and precious books for the Emperor, but also flattered his imperial pride by writing a number of texts on the royal lineage, including the *Epitome thesauri antiquitatum*, tracing Rudolf's forebears back to Julius Caesar. Strada was genuinely learned, however, and compiled an eleven-language dictionary, and produced works not only on antiquarianism but also on mechanics. His high position at court – Titian painted a very grand portrait of him – was no doubt sustained in part by the fact that his daughter Katarina was the bachelor Rudolf's long-time mistress, and bore him half a dozen children.[15]

As the years went on Rudolf sank deeper into melancholy and paranoia, and the courtiers tussling for position behind his throne took on much of the running of the Empire. Foremost among these was Wolfgang Rumpf, who as Chamberlain and then High Steward and President of the Privy Council made most of the Emperor's decisions. In 1599, however, Rudolf began to suspect that Rumpf was working against him, perhaps in league with the Spanish throne and its Prague faction, and dismissed him, then took him back, then fired him for good. Rudolf's favourite punishment for those he considered betrayers was to fling them into a dungeon and throw away the key. Poor Rumpf was to spend the rest of his life in prison, where a decade later another fallen courtier, the splendidly named Philipp Lang z Langenfelsu, a converted Jew and a dabbler in

[15] Their son, christened Julius Caesar after Rudolf's illustrious forebear, and variously known as Don Julius, Don César de Austria or Marquis Julio, was one of history's numerous Bluebeards. He found a mistress in the daughter of a barber-surgeon from Krumlov, but within a few months took seriously against her, so much so that after administering various beatings to the poor girl he flew into an uncontrollable rage one night and killed her and chopped up the body, afterwards ordering that the pieces be collected and wrapped in linen and given a solemn funeral. He is said to have died at Krumlov Castle at the age of twenty-three, already a wasted debauchee. How these monsters enliven history's duller pages!

alchemy, was to die a mysterious and violent death. It does not do to cross a Habsburg.

With Rumpf's abrupt and final departure the business of government virtually ground to a halt. Rudolf was given increasingly to sudden, unprovoked and terrible rages, which alternated with profound depressions. He kept entirely to the castle now, where he had the walkways and promenades covered in so that he might move about his twilight world unobserved. In his poem, 'Prague', Seifert writes:

Night towers over all
and through the box-trees of evergreen cupolas
the foolish emperor tiptoes away
into the magic gardens of his retorts
and in the halcyon air of rose-red evenings
rings out the tinkle of the glass foliage
as it is touched by the alchemists' fingers
as if by the wind.

In 1611 Rudolf's younger brother Matthias, whom he had always treated appallingly, called a meeting of the family in the Hofburg in Vienna. There were fears of a Protestant takeover of the imperial throne which Rudolf's slow decline had left unprotected. Matthias was named head of the House of Habsburg and declared Regent. He marched with an army to the gates of Prague, and on November 11th forced Rudolf to abdicate, leaving him with a pension, the castle on Hradčany, and, of course, his collections. Very soon, to his horror, Rudolf's tame African lion died, an event which according to an oracle would presage the death of its master. Rudolf submerged himself in drink, developed dropsy, and expired, no doubt painfully, on January 20th, 1612. For all his personal strangeness and the haplessness of his reign, the city on the Vltava mourned him, recognising him as a true spiritual son.

Who can guess the judgement of posterity? Searching the Internet for information on Rudolf, I was offered not Ripellino or Evans or Yates, but, mysteriously, the memoirs of an SS Kommandant at Auschwitz, the *Eddeades IV et V* of Plotinus, three taped episodes of the *Teletubbies*, and seven versions of *Rudolph the Red-Nosed Reindeer*. Thus does the glory fall.

3

THE PRAGUE ORGY

When I was a boy I fell in love with Eva Bartok. Eva was a film actress of the 1950s, whose real name was, or is – for all I know she may still be vigorously alive, over there in Budapest, or Beverly Hills, and I hope she is – Eva Ivanova Szöke. She was married four times, once to the actor Kurt Jürgens but never once to me, and was said to have had numerous lovers, among them Frank Sinatra – who denied he was the father of her only child – and, somewhat startlingly, the Marquess of Milford Haven. In 1959 she published her autobiography, *Worth Living For*, which I am disloyal enough not to have read. Her films include *The Crimson Pirate* (1952), the interestingly titled *Ten Thousand Bedrooms* (1957), and the one in which I best remember her, *Operation Amsterdam* (1959), with Peter Finch. Eva's dark and soulful brand of beauty was very much the look of her time; to me, she was a rich man's Juliette Gréco. In *Operation Amsterdam* I recall very black, shoulder-length hair and a thrillingly severe, straight fringe, a black polo-neck sweater tight enough across the bosom to make my adolescent gonads sizzle, and an equally tight skirt, of black leather – worthy of Marta, the Professor's wife – or so my fevered recollections insist. For a boy watching a matinée showing in a smoky cinema in the eternal afternoon of 1950s provincial Ireland, she was everything that the great world promised. To me, she was worth dying for.

Years later, when I began to travel beyond what was then the Iron Curtain and into Eastern Europe, I discovered that Eva was not unique. In fact, there were Eva Bartoks all over Hungary and Czechoslovakia, and probably all over the other Eastern Bloc countries I had not yet visited. Everywhere one looked, on the streets, in the trams, behind the counters of dowdy shops, there they were, Eva's sisters or cousins, just as dark and soulful and nearly as lovely as she, with that same faraway look in their sloe-black eyes, dreaming, as surely she must for long have dreamed, of the West and all its wonderful decadence. In my first days in Prague I moved through the streets in a state of low-grade anguish at the spectacle of so many beautiful women, not the glossy, soot-and-silver wraiths of the cinema screens of my youth, but palpably real persons, walking about unconcernedly, or hurrying to an assignation, or standing at a bus stop hunched over a cigarette, or, indeed, sitting together in a pair at a table under a plastic palm tree in a hotel lobby on the look-out for custom.

The first one of these fascinating creatures I got to speak to in circumstances that could be called in any way intimate was Kateřina – I have forgotten her surname, if I ever knew it – a freelance editor working at the time for a small Prague publishing house. I met her on my second visit to the city, again in winter. I had been to Kutná Hora to view, among other interesting sites, the famous Bone Chapel,[16] and when I came back in

[16] Kutná Hora lies some seventy kilometres east of Prague. The ossuary is situated a short way outside the town, in the Chapel of All Saints – it flies a flag sporting a skull and crossbones – dating from around 1400. The cemetery was a popular burial place, after a Cistercian abbot returning from the Crusades had spread a layer of soil from the Holy Land over it, and by the 1500s it had become so crowded that a Cistercian monk was given the task of disinterring the old residents to make way for new applicants. He gathered some 40,000 skeletons. Nearly four centuries later, in 1870, a local woodcarver, František Rindt, was hired, on who knows what ecclesiastical whim, to employ the bones to decorate the inside of All Saints. The result is one of the Czech Republic's more grisly tourist attractions. The centrepiece of the ossuary is a full-sized, working chandelier made from bones. There are bone crucifixion scenes, bone portraits, and a bone coat of arms of the

the afternoon there was a note waiting for me at my hotel from an old acquaintance, a Czech journalist named Jan. He wrote that he had heard I was in town – how, I wondered? – and that by coincidence another friend was also here, Philip, an American poet who ran a little magazine in a city in upper New York state, Syracuse, I think, or perhaps it was Albany. The three of us had first encountered each other some years before in wintry Madison, where we were attending a literary gathering at the University of Wisconsin. I liked Jan, a tall, thin, bearded, nervous young man with a tremor in his hands and a permanently worried expression – 'haunted' is the epithet that springs to mind. He was funny, in his sombre Czech way. I wondered then, as I do still, how he had managed to get a visa to travel to America, seemingly without difficulty, in those Cold War days of the Andropov interregnum. Was he an apparatchik, or its Czech equivalent? – not that I would have disapproved, particularly, for who can say what accommodations one might come to, given the circumstances and the

Schwartzenberg family, featuring, if I am not confusing my images, a bone raven plucking a bone eye – a ball joint – from the head of a bone Turk. Not surprisingly, the great Czech animator, Jan Švankmajer, made a short film on the subject, in black and white, featuring a lively jazz score. The Bone Chapel is a place of horrible fascination, and should be pulled down and given a decent burial.

necessity? He was witheringly critical of Gustav
Husák's horrible régime, yet, as I discovered one
drunken night at a party in someone's house
overlooking one of Madison's many lakes, he
was nevertheless a doctrinaire Marxist. In the
freezer in the kitchen we had found a bottle of
Stolichnaya, Jan and Philip and I, which we had
liberated from its Siberian cell – Jan declared it
the People's Vodka; we were already fatuously
tipsy – and as we sat in the gloaming at a picture
window, looking out at the frozen lake glimmering in ghostly moonlight and passing the bottle of
gelid, steely liquor from hand to hand and mouth
to mouth, Jan made a passionate speech in praise
of dialectical materialism, delivered, however, in
a low, urgent murmur, as if he were worried that
he might be overheard and arrested by the cam-
pus police, a not irrational fear, come to think of
it. The moment recalled for me other, similar
moments which I could not immediately place.
Next morning, though, feeling my way cau-
tiously through the fog of a vodka hangover, I
realised that what Jan reminded me of most was
those Irish Catholic priests of the post-Conciliar
1960s who had been to John XXIII's Rome and
come back to Dublin burning with reformist
zeal. One encountered them, these liberal zealots,
at parties much like this one, thrilled with them-

selves in the new dispensation; they too would drink too much, and late at night back one into a corner and, in tones similar to Jan's, breathe into one's ear the hot good news from the Vatican Council that Christ the Aquarian was in the ascendant. Of course, press them on dogma – contraception, sex before marriage, that kind of thing – and one struck against the old, iron rules. As many have remarked, Catholicism and Communism have much in common.

So now here we were again, the three of us, meeting up in another snowbound city. I had telephoned Jan and asked him to come to my hotel. He and Philip arrived together, but when I suggested a drink in the hotel bar Jan glanced about the lobby and shook his head and walked back into the street and hailed a taxi. It was twilight, and snow flurries were swirling in the pallid light of the street lamps. What was wrong with the hotel bar, I asked? Jan shrugged. 'Russians,' he said, reminding me of my first meeting with the Professor, and then made that odd, snuffly sound that I remembered from our previous acquaintanceship, half joyless laugh, half snort of pure disgust, which in turn, eerily, reminded me of Marta. According to Jan, I had managed to choose the hotel in Prague most favoured by Russian businessmen, Russian army

officers, and Russian spies. In the taxi Jan sat in
the front seat, talking to the driver – they seemed
to know each other – while in the back Philip and
I warily reminisced about that week we had spent
in each other's company in the Midwest. Philip,
Big Phil, was a large, unsteady man, hard-breath-
ing, bespectacled, with a footballer's shoulders
and thick, touchingly unhandy hands. He had
been more Jan's friend than mine – I think they
had known each other before Madison, for Philip
in his role as magazine editor had been a frequent
traveller to Prague and points east – and I always
felt he held me suspect in some never defined
way. Curious, these intermittent and far-flung
encounters into which life insists on leading us.
I have never been an adept of international relations. I envy those travellers who can drop in on
friends in all corners of the world at a moment's
notice and be at ease in their company as if they
had parted from them only yesterday. It was said
of Sir Alfred Beit, the diamond magnate and art
collector, that he kept his houses in England,
America and Ireland fully staffed and functioning
all year round, with food in the kitchens and
freshly laundered clothes in the wardrobes, so
that he and Lady Beit could travel luggageless
and walk in their front doors and take up their
Irish, English or American lives without breaking

stride. In a similar way, but without needing all that money, how nice it would be to meet up with old pals in New York, or London, or Prague, and not have to unpack the years that have passed since we last met. I always feel a constricting shyness when I encounter someone after a long absence, as if all that had happened to both of us in the intervening years had somehow to be accounted for, like a clandestine love affair discovered by one's spouse. So as Philip in his stertorous mumble interrogated me about my doings over the previous three years I felt myself as usual squirming evasively, with the result that we quickly fell into a silence that was aggrieved on his side and shamefaced on mine.

We were on our way to a café, the Slavia, it must have been, on the river down at the end of Národní Avenue, in the New Town. The snow was falling faster now, and as it came to a stop at traffic lights or negotiated tricky bends, the ancient taxi wallowed and yawed on the slippery, fresh surface, creaking, like a boat caught sideways in a rip tide, to the quiet amusement of our driver. In the East, in those days, snow did not carry the Dickensian, bells-and-holly promise that it does for us in the West, it was too chillingly suggestive of windswept, floodlit wastes and huddled huts and freezing figures lying swaddled in their rags on rows of bunks in the deep Arctic night. In Prague, snow was serious.

We were wafted into the café on a blast of icy air. The place was crowded but quiet. Heads were lifted and glances swept us swiftly, hope-fully, thorough as a policeman's hands checking us for what we might be carrying, then the eyes dropped back to books, or chessboards, or just the shadows under tables. We sat by a steamed window and drank bitter coffee and a peculiarly slimy liquor that the label on the bottle said was cognac. Talk among the three of us was desul-tory. Jan was distracted, and my reticence in the taxi obviously still rankled with Philip. I looked about. Since the 1920s the Slavia has been one of Prague's leading literary cafés. Kafka mentions it in his diaries, and Rilke used to take his evening coffee here, got up in spats and starched collar and white cotton gloves; it is the setting for some of his short stories, *Tales of Prague*. Seifert was an habitué, and even wrote a series of 'Slavia Poems'. The Slavia is not arranged after the Austro-Hungarian model, all dark old wood and cosy inwardness; it is more like the Caffè San Marco in Trieste, one of the world's great coffee houses, noisy, even a little rowdy, and somewhat higgledy-piggledy, with tables set too close to each other so that when you stand up, your chair back makes the customer behind you knock his front teeth against the rim of his espresso cup. Also, the Slavia looks not in but out, on to the quayside and the Vltava. In 1991 the café was closed for renovation, and stayed closed for seven years due to a leasing dispute between a consortium of Boston investors and the Film School next door. The President, Václav Havel, was among the many Praguers who loudly protested the closure; when eventually the Slavia reopened in 1998, Havel spoke of the saving of a national institution.

That night in the 1980s it seemed more like a national memorial. Who are the most numerous frequenters of public literary establishments, so-called? In the 1960s in Dublin I found no Behan or Kavanagh in McDaid's or Mulligan's, and when I was in Paris and walked past the Café Flore or the Deux Magots – what penniless young Irishman on his first Paris visit would dare venture inside such frighteningly suave and expensive places? – I saw a lot of American tourists, but no sign of Sartre or de Beauvoir hard at work over their *cahiers* and *cafés*. The customers in the Slavia that night did not look likely *littérateurs* to me. They were young, poorly dressed and bored, or middle-aged and dowdy; only in the elderly among them, I thought, was there discernible the still-surviving glow of an intellectual spark. I remember one night in Dublin in 1987 arguing with Joseph Brodsky and Susan Sontag about yet another letter they and other East Coast luminaries had written to the *New York Review of Books* protesting the imprisonment of intellectuals in the Soviet Union. Did they ever, I demanded – the wine was flowing, and I could hardly see Brodsky behind the clouds of cigarette smoke in which he was forever enveloped – did they, he and his American friends, ever think to protest about the imprisonment of a Russian street sweeper, or charlady, some poor nobody who had not even written a subversive poem but still had ended up in prison? Sontag was adamant on the need to keep pecking away at the vast repressive machine that was the Soviet Union, and no doubt she was right. Brodsky, however, a fine, just and courageous man, conceded that, yes, 'we do tend to look after our own.' Recently I read a memorial tribute to Brodsky, who died of a heart attack in 1996 at the age of only fifty-six, by the Russian essayist and fiction writer, Tatyana Tolstaya. She wrote of how she had urged him after 1989 to return to Russia – a thing he was superstitiously unwilling to do: she quoted a poem written in his youth in which he prophesied *Neither country nor churchyard will I choose/I'll come to Vasilevsky Island to die* – so that all those who had revered him as their spokesman when he was in exile might have the comfort of seeing him back amongst them in St Petersburg, even if it meant risking a visit to Vasilevsky Island. 'What about all those little old ladies of the intelligentsia,' Tolstaya had reminded him, 'your readers, all the librarians, museum staff, pensioners, communal apartment dwellers who are afraid to go out into the communal kitchen with their chipped teakettle? The ones who stand in the back rows at philharmonic concerts, next to the columns, where the tickets are cheaper?' Tolstaya was right. We know about the great ones, the Solzhenitsyns, the Brodskys, the Sakharovs, but when, even in those dark days before the Fall of the Wall, did we think about the 'little old ladies of the intelligentsia', those sustainers of the spark, those no less heroic guardians of the light?

Philip had arrived that day from Bucharest, where he had been seeing one of his dissident poets – although the adjective is superfluous, since to write poetry in Romania then was automatically to dissent. I was interested to hear a first-hand account of life there, suspecting, as so many of us in the West suspected, that reports of the gaudy excesses of the Ceaușescu régime must

be in part at least inspired by the American
Central Intelligence Agency. Philip was there to
enlighten me, however. He is one of those wised-
up people, is Phil, who see themselves both as
social outsiders – dissidents, if you like – and as
players strenuously engaged in the great game of
world politics. Whatever you vaguely believe,
whatever fuzzy opinion you may hold, whatever
way you choose to account for world-historical
events, Philip can be depended upon to show you
how fatuous and shallow you are in your grasp of
reality, how hopelessly limited in your thinking.
In Phil's version, everything that happens is either
the innocent-seeming tip, glistening there in the
sun, of an immense, malignant iceberg, or a
deliberately manufactured smokescreen behind
which a secret inferno is raging. Nothing, for
Phil, is as it seems, and he has the inside information. Yes, all that I have heard about Ceauşescu
and his doings is correct, Phil can tell me. In fact, I
do not know the half of it. When Phil was in
Bucharest, Ceauşescu was returning from one of
his many triumphal progresses through the
world's capitals. To mark his homecoming, or
so Philip swore, a full-sized replica of the Arc de
Triomphe, made from plywood, or maybe even
cardboard, had been erected on the road along
which the President would travel on his way in

from the airport. In the city centre the boulevards along which the President's motorcade would pass were emptied of onlookers – that is, possible troublemakers – by squads of security police in ankle-length leather overcoats and slouch hats, just like the Gestapo, on whom, or on movie versions of whom, they had probably modelled themselves. Yes, typewriters were licensed, and could be confiscated without warning. The Ceauşescu family ran the country like a mafia, for their own aggrandisement and to fill their secret Swiss bank accounts. All this was true, all this and more. Jan, making abstract designs with his fingertip in a pinch of spilled salt on the table, nodded gloomily: yes, yes, all true. 'Ceauşescu is a vampire,' he said with a sigh, 'his wife too, that bitch. Between them they have brought Romania back to the Middle Ages.' The Russians knew it, of course, knew how bad things were, but what could they do? 'If they invade, take over the government, the Americans will howl; let matters go on as they are, the country will explode. Either way, is a disaster.' Big Phil, however, was shaking his big head slowly and smiling his pitying smile. How could we be so dumb? Could we not see the true situation? The fact was, Reagan and his people were Ceauşescu's real sponsors and protectors. This made even Jan sit up. Phil looked from one of us to the other, still smiling, still shaking his head, like a teacher regarding two of his most favoured pupils on one of their less brilliant days. 'Listen,' he said, and when Phil said 'listen' in that soft, patient tone you knew you were about to get the real stuff, the lowdown, the insider's inside information. 'It's simple. What is the worst advertisement for Marxist-Leninism, atheistic communism and the Soviet so-called Union?' He opened his hands and showed us two broad, soft, pink palms. 'Romania!' Ceauşescu was a precious asset for Reagan and the CIA. The Agency, as Phil familiarly, almost fondly, called it, regularly ferried Ceauşescu's top security people to a base in Turkey for training in state-of-the-art – it was the first time I had heard the phrase – anti-insurrectionist techniques, developed in the jungles of South America. The Israelis too were involved. 'The Israelis!' Phil cried, with a harsh laugh. 'The frigging *Israelis*!' He knew for a fact that Ceauşescu had commissioned an Israeli arms firm to provide him with a fleet of attack helicopters specifically designed to tackle urban guerrilla warfare. He reached out and traced a triangle in the spilled salt on the table, cutting through Jan's designs.

'There it is,' he said, 'the axis: Washington, Tel

Aviv, Bucharest.' Then he sat back and folded his arms.

Jan, I could see, shared my doubts about all this, frowning into the middle distance and running his fingers through his scant beard. Neither of us, however, was willing to speak up. It is the nature of secret knowledge such as Phil claimed to possess that it is unverifiable, and therefore unchallengeable. Why had we heard nothing of Reagan supporting Ceauşescu, of the CIA training Romanian security police, of Israel supplying weapons to Bucharest? Because it's all a secret, of course, stupid! And it might all be true, too. The CIA had tried to kill Castro with an exploding cigar. One of Jimmy Carter's people had gone to Teheran bearing a cake and a copy of the Koran as gifts for the mad mullahs with whom he was to negotiate. Anything is possible.

The snow outside was turning to sleet, falling slantwise sluggishly in the light of the street lamps and extinguishing itself in the dark surface of the river. Although night had fallen it was still early, and Phil had the ominous look of a reality instructor warming to his task. Then Jan asked him if he had spoken to Kateřina since his arrival in Prague. He shrugged. Now it was Jan's turn to smile and shake his head. He fished in the pockets of his jeans and came up with a coin and went to the telephone beside the gasping espresso machine. Who is Kateřina, I asked? Philip shrugged again. 'A girl,' he said. He looked vexed; he had hardly begun to tap into his store of secret knowledge, the great world's arcana. After a brief and what seemed furtive conversation on the telephone Jan came back to the table. Kateřina was at home, and was having a party, and we were invited. A girl. We paid and left.

Praguers are the most circumspect of city dwellers. Travellers on trams and in the metro carefully remove the dust jackets of books, no matter how innocuous, that they have brought to read on the journey; some will even make brown-paper covers to hide the titles of paperbacks. Understandable, of course in a city for so long full of informers, and old habits die hard. Likewise, our brief journey to Kateřina's apartment had the air of the credits sequence of a 1960s espionage movie. First there was Jan on the telephone in the café cupping his hand over the receiver and raising a protective shoulder to the room as if he thought there might be a lip reader on the premises, then we were outside, three hunched figures on an empty avenue, walking clichés, shouldering against the wind and the darkness and the gusts of flabby sleet, spies who went out into the cold for a rendezvous with *the woman called Kateřina*. After we had waited for a numbing ten minutes at a corner rank an ancient taxi wheezed up and, eager as eskimos, we piled into its leather-and-cigarette-smoke-smelling back seat, huddling together for warmth.

Taxis are another of Prague's mysteries. They seem to congregate and swim in protective shoals, like a species of large, unlovely, shy sea creature. Until 1989 they were run by the Prague Transport Corporation, which meant they were dependable to some degree, but now they are all privately owned, with the results that one might expect. It is impossible to flag down a taxi, if you are a foreigner, or at least I have never succeeded in doing so. There must be a set of coded signals known only to native Praguers. Often I have stood on the pavement wanly waving as cab after cab plunged past, every one of them empty, only to have some leather-jacketed fellow with the regulation drooping moustache step nimbly past me and, like an expert bidder at an auction, lift one finger, or flex an eyebrow, at which a taxi I had not even seen approach would slew across three lanes of blaring traffic and pull to a smoking halt at the kerb with its back door already swinging open. Nowadays one is warned off taxis altogether. On my most recent visit to the city the first thing I saw when I entered my hotel room was a notice from the manager cheerily assuring me – 'Dear Honoured Guest!' – that if I were to hail a cab in the street I would almost certainly be charged an exorbitant rate, with the additional hint that this would like be the least of the evils that would befall me; instead, I should ask reception to call a car from their own private service. I assumed this was a piece of strategic exaggeration on the part of the hotel, but when I checked with a diplomat from the Irish embassy he told me how a few nights before he had taken a taxi from the railway station to his home and even though the meter registered 600 crowns the driver insisted on charging 6,000. Did you pay, I asked him? 'Oh, I paid,' he said grimly, breathing heavily down his nostrils. It seemed best to drop the subject.

I heard Kateřina sneeze before I saw her. She lived on Slezská Avenue, on the eastern side of the city, in a big, blank apartment block behind one of those grey, many-windowed cliff-faces so characteristic of Eastern Europe.[17] There was an

[17] However, on that last visit to Prague I had a drink at the Slavia – if it is changed after its famous interval of renovation I failed to detect the alterations, for good or ill – and afterwards, when I was leaving the café, my memory having been jogged, perhaps, by the cold and sleety night, I telephoned my hotel and they sent a car and I went to Slezská Avenue in search of the building where Kateřina had lived, but could not find it. In fact, the avenue was nothing like the

open entranceway of grey concrete where a naked bulb was burning, and a clanging grey metal door which Kateřina had to use both hands to haul open. She was, indeed, a very Eva, and was even wearing a tight black sweater with a polo neck, and black leather boots. She was very beautiful, with a sharp, heart-shaped face and thin, long, pale hands and long, slender legs. Particularly appealing were those deep shadows, of a pale plum shade, under her eyes, so characteristic of Eastern European women. She gave a loud, liquid snuffle, and smiled. The wings of her nose were red and raw, and she was clutching a sodden tissue. Jan and Philip kissed her on the cheek. With me she shook hands. 'Oh,' she said, 'forgib me, I hab such a code.'

Her apartment consisted of a single, enormous room furnished sparsely with a lopsided sofa, some straight-backed chairs, a mahogany table with carved legs – lugubrious survivor of a bygone bourgeois age – an overflowing bookcase, and an elaborate stereo system housed in an upright black perspex cabinet. There was a tiny

grim canyon I thought I remembered, but a rather pretty, not very wide thoroughfare with fine nineteenth-century architecture, and a park running parallel one street down. Yet in my memory I distinctly see that big grey pile, the bare bulb, the big metal door. Sometimes one is led to wonder if memory is a faculty of deception rather than recollection.

fireplace with a tiled surround, the fireless grate already half filled with wadded paper hankies. The only source of heating that I could see in the room was a small hot-air blower, an oddly animate-seeming appliance that squatted froglike in the middle of the floor, its mouth wide open and its engine whirring at full though inadequate blast. Obviously Jan and Phil and I were much too early, for not only were there no other guests present, but there were no visible signs of any preparations for the party. Kateřina turned the sofa sideways-on to the fireplace while Jan and Philip brought forward the straight-backed chairs. As this was my first visit, the rules of hospitality insisted, it seemed, that I must sit on the sofa, with the result that I spent the entire evening in a vaguely helpless, semi-recumbent sprawl, peering up waiflike at the others perched on their grown-up chairs. Every so often I would drag myself upright, wriggling and grunting, only to subside again inexorably into the bumpy upholstery wallowing around me like quicksand. In a far corner of the room there was a tall refrigerator, big as a packing crate, from which Kateřina fetched a bottle of freezing wine, Moravian, slightly fizzy, and sickly sweet, which we drank from tumblers. At regular intervals Kateřina would be overcome by a sneezing fit – really,

for such a slight and delicately made girl she
sneezed with remarkable force – at the end of
which she would blow her nose violently, as if to
punish it for its betrayals, crush the tissue in her
fist and with rueful aplomb toss it into the grate
to join the steadily growing slushy white mountain of its fellows. What did we talk about? Philip
rehearsed his Romanian adventures, and Jan
gave us a long, rambling account of a fist fight
he had got himself into late one drunken night
outside a bar in a small town somewhere in
windy Wisconsin. The point of the story was
that his opponent turned out to be a second-
generation Pole whose parents, old-style Marx-
ists, had been imprisoned in the McCarthy era.
When this bond was discovered, Jan and his new
friend went back into the bar and spent the rest of
the night drinking vodka and discussing Polish
politics. 'Of course,' Philip said when Jan had
finished his tale, 'Lech Wałesa is in the pay of the
KGB, as everybody knows.'

I was aware of a growing, mild distress, which
presently I identified as hunger: I had not eaten
since breakfast time. Still there was no sign of the
party getting under way. We had finished the
wine, and after a long and sneeze-interrupted
search Kateřina turned up a half bottle of slivovitz which she had brought back from a trip years

before to Dubrovnik. Plum brandy has not been
nor will ever be my tipple, but I drank it grate-
fully that night. Hunger and cold and the hum-
ming of the heater had combined to set up a
throbbing ache in my temples. I thought of my
hotel with its murky little bar, and the cavernous
dining room that could be filled to bursting with
roistering Muscovites for all I cared, if only I
could be there, at a corner table, with my book
and a bottle; I even found myself thinking wist-
fully of a nice plate of smoked pork with sauerkraut and a steaming triorch of potato dumplings
on the side. The doorbell sounded, interrupting
my reverie. Kateřina went out, and Jan and Philip
looked at each other expressionlessly for a moment and then suddenly both gave a spluttering
laugh. Was Kateřina the object of their amusement, or was there something else entirely going
on of which I was ignorant? There is a facial
expression which I have developed over the years
to put on in U.S.A. – Unmanageable Situations
Abroad – a sort of misty, ultra-bland half smile
meant to indicate that although I do not understand what is going on, usually because of language difficulties, I am perfectly willing, if
everyone is laughing, to have the joke explained,
even if it is on me, or, if everyone is scowling, to
apologise if I have inadvertently caused offence

by word or deed; or simply to suggest in a quiet way that I am not as idiotic as I might seem. Many years ago, when I was a young man and on one of my first ventures into foreign parts, I was at a party in Rotterdam, sitting on the floor trying to impress a Dutch beauty – trying, indeed, to see if before the night was out I might be invited to venture further into foreign parts – who asked me, in a particularly long lull in an already halting conversation, if I liked Geneva, or at least that is what I understood her to be asking. I gave the world-weary shrug of a jaded traveller and said that I had never been to that city. Blonde Beauty gave a hearty laugh, and called to her friends to come and share the joke. She had been asking me not for my opinion of Rousseau's birthplace, but if I would care to have a drink from the bottle of gin standing on the floor beside her. I do not think my measure of myself as a sophisticate every quite recovered from that incident.

So when Kateřina came back into the room leading a middle-aged couple whom she introduced only as Rosa and Alex, I adopted my U.S.A. expression as I waited warily to find out who they might be. From their general and not unappealing shabbiness and vague air of distraction I took them for intellectuals of a

minor sort, university lecturers, perhaps, or
schoolteachers, or even writers. Rosa was one
of those women who at fifty retain a vivid image
of what they looked like at twenty, the visible
ghost of their younger selves still haunting them
in the slenderness of a neck, the delicacy of an
ankle, the erotic tenderness of a smile. She was
tall and attractively gaunt, with the head of one
of Modigliani's less dim-seeming models. She
wore an enormous fur coat with bald patches,
which at first she refused to take off, complaining
of the cold, and indeed the pale hand she laid
briefly in mine had the chill, slack feel of a small,
exquisite, fine-boned creature that had recently
frozen to death. Her greying hair was tied behind
in a bun from which fine wisps kept floating free
and straying about her face in an underwater
way, making me think, disconcertingly, of poor
Ophelia submerged in her brook under that
willow. Alex, on the other hand, was pure Che-
khov. Tall like Rosa, and extraordinarily thin, he
had the long, greyish face of a suffering ascetic; in
my memory he wears pince-nez, but no doubt
memory is being fanciful. He had very large,
splayed feet, and was in need of a shave; the
sprinkle of silver glitter in the stubble on his chin
and in the hollows of his cheeks was peculiarly
affecting, a token of the dishevelled old age that

was awaiting him. Rosa sat beside me on the sofa, perched on the front edge of the cushion and turned a little sideways with her lovely hands folded in her lap. She had changed from Ophelia now into Edith Sitwell, only less pursed and pinched. She kept heaving fluttery, troubled little sighs, and seemed at every moment about to burst into a litany of complaint, or to cry out in tragic supplication. I would have thought she was on the brink of some terrible collapse of the spirit or the mind had not the others in the room seemed quite accustomed to what I took to be the signs of her distress. Alex was standing at the bookcase with his hands clasped behind his back, frowning at the titles through those pebble lenses I have imagined for him. He had not spoken a word since entering the room, not even when I, the stranger – Jan and Philip he seemed to know – was introduced to him, yet his silence seemed not rudeness so much as a kind of consideration, as if everything that he had to say had been said already, to everyone, and he was too kindly to think of burdening us with repetition.

Kateřina meanwhile had rinsed two cups at the sink and was pouring out the last of the slivovitz for the newcomers. Alex at first tried to refuse, screwing his lips into a smile and shaking his head, his courtly hands lifted and spread palm outward at his chest, but Kateřina insisted, and in the end he took the cup and gave a little bow and – or do I imagine it again? – clicked his heels. Rosa knocked back her dram in one go, expertly, with no more it seemed than a light intake of breath, and gazed before her with a frown of concentration, like that of a communicant on the way back from the altar rails. While she had greeted Philip warmly enough, I had the impression, from the way she angled her shoulder in his direction, that she disapproved of Jan. For his part he was taking no notice of her, in a determinedly pointed way. All this, of course, I found baffling, and assumed I was missing some explanatory link between the people in the room. I had still been given no indication of who precisely Alex and Rosa were. Party guests? – but could this be called a party? Relations of Kateřina's, an uncle and aunt, perhaps, or parents, even? Talk was desultory, and, when it was directed at Alex and Rosa, all in Czech. Alex had still said nothing. I drained the last, burning drop of slivovitz in my tumbler. Now all the drink was gone. I sneaked a look at my watch. It was half past eight.

I wish I could say that at that moment suddenly the door burst open and a crowd of half-drunk Praguers came in singing, waving bottles and with sausages sticking out of their pockets, and that I was swept up from the lumpy sofa and made to dance until dawn. And that at dawn, Alex and Rosa having left long ago, Kateřina, laughing, pushed Jan and Big Phil out the door, and turned and took my hand and led me to her bed, where we lay down together, and I was Peter Finch and she was Eva Bartok, and . . . and . . . and . . . But nothing like that happened. Kateřina made coffee, and Rosa was at last persuaded to take off her coat, and Jan told another incoherent story from his time in America, laughing at his own jokes; I had not noticed before how crazy Jan's laugh could sound. Then there was a long period of silence as we drank our coffee. Kateř-ina, her cold worsening by the minute, sat hunched before the hot-air heater, gasping softly and juicily blowing her poor, raw nose and squishing the tissues in her fist and lobbing them into the by now overflowing grate. Rosa said something to her in Czech, a rebuke, it sounded like, and she scowled and flung herself from her chair and stalked across the room to the galley kitchen and rattled the coffee pot angrily on the stove, and sneezed. Rosa threw her eyes to hea-ven and stood up and went to her, and they began to argue in tones of hushed fury. Jan looked at Philip, who shrugged. Alex now provided the first, the only, faint interest of the evening when, in a polite attempt to distract attention from the squabbling women, he came and took Rosa's place beside me on the sofa and with a sort of wistful leer asked in a perfect imitation of a Dublin accent if I would 'fancy coming out for a pint'. It turned out that he was, or had been – most academics that I met in the city in those days seemed to be unemployed – a professor of Anglo-Irish literature. He had been to Ireland. Dreamily he named the shrines he had visited: 'Eccles Street . . . Thoor Ballylee . . . the Aran Islands . . .' He had met Brendan Behan. Certainly, I said, you must have gone out for a pint with *him?* But Brendan, it seemed, had already drunk many pints, and fallen asleep at the bar. Irish people were very nice, Alex said, very friendly. The librarian at the National Library had told him a joke about James Joyce which he had not quite understood – 'Can you tell me, please, what is a piss artist?' – and in Sligo an ancient boatman had assured him that no one in the area had ever heard of the Lake Isle of Innisfree, and that when tourists asked him to take them there he would row them out to Rat Island instead. I said it was true, that when Yeats himself in old age went to look for Innisfree he could not find it. Professor Alex laughed softly, shaking his head. I asked if

he had meant it, about going with him for a pint;
I tried not to sound desperate. He laughed again,
regretfully this time, a very Uncle Vanya sprung
to melancholy life. There was no Guinness to be
had in Prague. I said I did not mind, that I would
drink anything. This for some reason he found
very funny, and winked at me, and punched me
softly on the upper arm, wag that I was.

By now the argument behind us had waned,
and Rosa came back, looking offended and cross,
and put on her fur coat. Alex said something to
her concerning me, I suspect recounting my un-
intentional witticism about my drinking habits,
and she gave me a wry and, I thought, faintly
pitying smile. Alex gravely shook hands with me,
and stood up and followed Rosa to the door.
There they both paused, somewhat melodrama-
tically, I thought – Rosa very Sitwellian now –
and looked back at Kateřina, who uttered a word
angrily under her breath but nevertheless went
and accompanied them out, leaving the door
open behind her. We listened to their footsteps
receding down the stairs. 'Jesus Christ,' Philip
said, 'and I think my folks are bad.' Oh, I said, so
Rosa and Alex were Kateřina's parents? Philip
looked at me and then at Jan, and they did their
spluttery laugh again. I heard the front door
opening below, and Kateřina and her putative

parents saying their strained goodnights. A draught came in from the landing, bringing a strangely heart-piercing smell of snow. When Kateřina came back she would not look at either of the men, but went to the sink and began bad-temperedly to wash the crockery. Philip said something to her and she shrugged and answered nothing, keeping her back turned. Jan stood up and flexed an eyebrow at me and at the door, putting on his leather jacket. The party, it seemed, was over. I took up my coat, expecting Philip to do the same, but Philip, Big Phil, was staying, it seemed. We shook hands, he and I, and said we must get together again, in Dublin, or New York, or Saratoga Springs. Kateřina came to the door again to say goodbye. I leaned forward to kiss her cheek but she sneezed, and stepped back, smiling an apology.

In the street the snow lay thick; Alex's and Rosa's footprints were already almost filled. Jan stuck his hands into the pockets of his jacket and together we headed into the swirling night. I asked about Phil and Kateřina. Jan lifted a shoulder and turned down the corners of his mouth. 'She thinks he will bring her to New York, give her a job, make her a big-shot.' And will he? I asked. He glanced at me sideways, his eyes narrowed against the flying snow, and grinned . . .

Why have I remembered that night, and with such clarity, such vividness? Nothing, like something, can happen anywhere, Philip Larkin bitterly observes. Yet those particular nothings that happened in Kateřina's big, dim, cold room are somehow the quintessence for me of Prague before the revolution of 1989. The occasion had that particular quality – at once ordinary and mysterious, mundane and enigmatic, dull and yet bizarre – which for the visiting Westerner characterised the lives of these captive people. For that is what they were, captives, held in the prison of a vast, irresistible, wholly philistine system. The driving force of dissidents, especially the *émigrés*, from Solzhenitsyn on the far right to Joseph Brodsky on the cheerful left, was anger, pure fury, at the unrelenting and mindless effrontery of the Soviet régime. However, in Praguers such as Jan, and Kateřina and her parents, if they were her parents, what one sensed was not so much outrage as the aftermath of outrage, a kind of weariness, and boredom, and restless dissatisfaction. Kateřina was tired of the pettiness of her life, the huge empty room and the ineffective heater, the tumblers in the sink, the ill-stocked fridge, the draught on the stairs. She wanted colour, excitement, risk; like Marta the Professor's wife before her, she wanted America and all that America represented. I wonder if Phil ever did bring her there. I would prefer to think of her escaping on her own terms. Nowadays, when I come across an Eva lookalike doing some menial job in New York, or London, or Dublin – one such, a very beautiful one, with those irresistible dark shadows under her eyes, serves behind the counter in the frozen goods section of my local Asian food store, her long, slender hands rubbed raw and her shapely legs already varicose-veined – and wonder how she can bear such thankless work, I think of Kateřina, in her weary desperation. I think of Rosa, too, and wordless Alex, and of Marta and the Professor, and of others whom I knew, and the many others I did not know, all those damaged lives. I hope they are happier now, the ones who lived long enough to see the fell Calibans undone, yet always I hear the echo of my friend Zdeněk's sad complaint: 'Too late! Too late for me!'

4

GREAT DANE, LITTLE DOG

The once Danish, now Swedish, island of Hveen, or Hven, or simply Ven – let us choose a middle course and call it Hven – situated in the Øresund southeast of Helsingør, Hamlet's Elsinore, is 400 miles distant from Prague, as the seagull flies. The name is said to derive from that of Hvenild, maid-in-waiting to the Lady Grimmel, ruler of the island in the times before time, who is reputed to have murdered her two brothers, one of whom had got Hvenild with child. When Ranke, Hvenild's boy, grew up, he cast his auntie into a dungeon, where she would starve to death, and set himself in her place as the true lord of the isle. Later, in the thirteenth century, a party of Vikings, led by the Monty Pythonesque Eric the Priest-Hater, stopped off at Hven to do some marauding, in the course of which they destroyed four castles, possibly those that Lady Grimmel had built, at Nordburg, Sönderborg, Karlshög and Hammer. Through the following sleepy centuries the island lay at peace save for the violent winter storms that whistled down the Sound. And then, in 1576, there arrived on the rocky shore a large, imposing figure with flowing moustaches and a wedge of silver and gold alloy set into the bridge of his damaged nose, to whom King Frederick of Denmark had granted the island as a gift whereon to build what would become the great observatory of Uraniborg, one of the middling wonders of the Renaissance world.

Tycho Brahe was born in 1546 into the highest reaches of the Danish nobility. The Brahes had been among the first of Denmark's noble families to reject Catholicism in favour of the reformed religion. Tycho's paternal grandfather, Tyge Brahe, died at the siege of Malmö in 1523 defending the Lutheran cause that would bring the Reformation to Denmark, while Tyge's brother Axel had the honour of carrying the sceptre at the coronation of the militant Lutheran King Christian III in 1537. When Tycho Brahe was two years old, he was abducted from his parents' castle at Knudstrup, in what is now southern Sweden, by his uncle Jørgen Brahe and his wife

Inger Oxe (wives in Denmark then kept their maiden names after marriage). Mysteriously, Tycho's parents made scant protest at this piece of inter-family high-handedness, despite the fact that Tycho's twin, a boy, had died at birth;[18] it seems that Jørgen put it to Tycho's father that since he already had another son, while he and his wife were childless, it was only right that he should share his bounty. Tycho himself in later life was sanguine in the matter, saying only that Jørgen and Inger had supported him generously on their estate at Tostrup and treated him as their own son.

The Brahes were a warrior clan, but happily, through his kidnapping, Tycho came under the influence of a very different family. The Oxes, his Aunt Inger's people, put a high value on learning and culture. Inger Oxe's brother Peder was a man of great influence in Denmark, a kingmaker and member of the Council of the Realm. Inger shared many of her brother's intellectual interests, and was something of a thinker in her own right. For years she conducted a lively correspondence with the sister of the Danish King

[18] When as an adult Tycho was at last told by his mother that he had a dead twin brother he seems to have been deeply affected, and wrote a Latin poem which he set in the mouth of the dead child, who looked down on the living mortal with compassion: *He dwells on earth, while I dwell on Olympus.*

Frederick, Princess Anne of Denmark/Saxony, noted for her work in alchemy, even though alchemy was an almost exclusively male pursuit, not least because of the danger a woman ran of being accused of witchcraft for dabbling in the dark art.[19] No doubt Inger was a strong force in her nephew's education. After grammar school he first of all attended the University of Copenhagen – motto: 'He looks up to the light of heaven' – and after three years there moved on to study at Leipzig. As Tycho's latest biographer Victor E. Thoren puts it, 'When the time came to take the Grand Tour that had become a standard feature of the education of Danish aristocrats, Tycho followed the path of the Billes and Oxes to foreign universities, rather than the path of the Brahes to foreign wars.'

He was also a student for a time at Wittenberg, Luther's Alma Mater, but an outbreak of plague sent him scurrying north for safety to Rostock. It was at Rostock that he witnessed a lunar eclipse, on October 28th, 1566; Tycho, after careful study of the phenomenon, concluded that it presaged the death of the Turkish sultan, Suleiman the Great, and was unwise enough to publish a poem in Latin hexameters announcing the pend-

---

[19] Johannes Kepler's mother was branded a witch, for little more than the peddling of herbal remedies.

ing event. Shortly afterwards, word came that Suleiman had indeed died – six months before the eclipse. What did follow the eclipse was not a death but a disfigurement. A couple of months later, at a Christmas party, Tycho got into a violent argument with another Danish student staying in Rostock, Manderup Parsberg, a distant cousin of the Brahes, who may well have been mocking Tycho over the embarrassing Suleiman prophecy. The pair went outside to settle the matter with their broadswords. In the duel, Tycho received a blow to the face that hacked a large notch out of the bridge of his nose. He was lucky not to have died, from infection if not the sword cut itself, and spent a painful convalescence. When he returned home to Denmark, he fashioned a prosthesis for himself of gold and silver blended to a flesh colour, kept in place by means of an adhesive salve a supply of which he carried with him always in a little silver box. This precious nosepiece was, it seems, reserved for 'dress' occasions, while a copper one was used for ordinary daywear.

From an early age Tycho had been fascinated by astronomy, and as a student at Leipzig he 'bought astronomical books secretly, and read them in secret'; obviously the science of the stars was not an interest that the tankard-banging

Brahes would have approved, although his Aunt Inger was probably quietly encouraging. At the age of seventeen Tycho was already testing the accuracy, or otherwise, usually otherwise, of the various star charts drawn up by Ptolemy of Alexandria, who at the time was still one of the most revered astronomical authorities, or the more recent Prussian Tables devised according to the Copernican system. Tycho's measuring equipment consisted of nothing more than a little globe of the heavens, 'no bigger than a fist', and a taut length of string, which he would hold up against the night sky and align with a planet and two stars, then check the position of the planet according to the positions of the stars on the celestial globe.

Tycho's passion for accuracy was the mark of his greatness as a scientist. He was not a theorist of the first rank, such as Copernicus, for example, or Kepler, or Isaac Newton, nor was he Galileo's equal as a technologist of genius. But he did recognise the paramount necessity of making and recording accurate observations. In Leipzig he had bought an astronomical radius, which, although little more than a calibrated wooden cross-staff, was a far more sophisticated version of the taut-string device. However, the radius allowed for measurements accurate only

to one degree of arc, while Tycho was after
minute-of-arc accuracy – and a minute of arc
is one-sixtieth of a degree.[20] In Augsburg, to
where his European wanderings brought him
in the spring of 1596, he was chatting to a friend
in the street one day, telling him of his urgent
need for a bigger and better instrument, and by a
lucky chance was overheard by a local business-
man and amateur astronomer. This philanthropist – Paul Hainzel: every good man deserves to
be named – put up the money for the building of a
mighty oak-and-brass *quadrans maximus*, or
great quadrant, five and a half metres in radius
and so massive it took forty men to set it in place.
Even if the instrument proved less successful than
Tycho had hoped – the effort involved in wield-
ing the monster meant that for practical reasons
it could not be used more than once a night – its
renown brought Tycho to the attention of the
scientific world, and made his reputation as an
astronomer.

The data that Tycho accumulated over some
thirty-five years of stargazing – without, we must

---

[20] I could try to explain angular separation, degrees and minutes of
arc, etc., but it would be confusing for you and tedious for me;
besides, I am not as sure of my grasp of these matters as I like to
pretend. Those thirsting for knowledge might consult Appendix 1 of
Kitty Ferguson's book *The Nobleman and His Housedog*, which
provides a brief and not unclear explication of these matters.

never forget, the benefit of a telescope, which had not yet been invented – were the basis upon which Johannes Kepler would institute a cosmological revolution. Newton a century later would say that he had been able to see so far because he stood on the shoulders of giants,[21] and it was upon Brahe's broad yoke that the diminutive Kepler perched to peer into the shining depths of space. It was the purity and dependability of Brahe's data which made Kepler lick his chops and brought him trotting up to Prague in the notable year 1600 in hopes of being thrown a bone or two from the great Dane's star tables. Kepler himself was a less than perfect technician. For one thing, he suffered from double vision, a grave handicap, surely, for an astronomer. Also, he was no more interested in the actual disposition of the heavens than was Copernicus, who in his long lifetime took only half a dozen star readings. It was not the appearance of things that preoccupied Kepler and Copernicus, but the higher reality lying behind appearance.[22]

[21] Not as generous a tribute as it sounds: most Newton scholars now accept that he was aiming a cruel gibe at his rival Robert Hooke, an undersized hunchback.

[22] Before Kepler, all that was required of astronomers was that any planetary theory they propounded should 'save the phenomena', as the phrase had it – i.e., the theory was sound so long as it accounted for the movements of the planets as recorded from earth, and was not expected to be a picture of how things are in reality. 'Although it

John Banville

Not so Tycho Brahe. Before he was out of his teens he had, as he said himself, 'got accustomed to distinguishing all the constellations of the sky.' The truth of this modestly expressed claim is attested by his discovery on the evening of November 11th, 1572, of a 'new star'. At the time he was living at Herrevad Abbey, a converted Cistercian monastery not far from his family home at Knudstrup, in what is now southern Sweden. Walking back from his alchemical laboratory to supper at the abbey, he was stopped on the spot by the sight, directly above his head – those old astronomers must have had a permanent crick in their necks – of a light in the sky, near the constellation of Cassiopeia, which had not been there before. Modern astronomers have concluded that the 'new star' was probably a supernova, a huge explosion deep in space caused by the collapse of a 'white dwarf' under the force of its own gravity. Curiously, the records Tycho made of his sightings of the star over a period of weeks are the only observations of his to have been lost. Perhaps an explanation of this

would be incorrect to say that people like Ptolemy and Copernicus never pondered such causal questions, their primary concern was to describe and predict where heavenly bodies were positioned and the patterns of their movements, not to answer what *caused* them to be where they were and to move in certain patterns and at certain speeds and distances.' (Ferguson, *The Nobleman and His House-dog*) carelessness is the fact that it was at this time that he met the woman who was destined to share his life, as the old books used to put it. Kirsten Jørgensdatter was 'a woman of the people from Knudstrup village', that is, a commoner. As such, she was not a person a Brahe could marry. Nevertheless, she was the one for Tycho, and he stayed loyal to her until his death, fathering on her a brood of more or less troublesome children. Although such liaisons were not uncommon, one wonders what the noble Brahes thought of young Tycho's *slegfred*, or common law, wife. According to Brahe's first biographer, Pierre Gassendi, 'all of Tycho's relatives were very disturbed by the diminished esteem the family suffered because of Kirsten's low birth, so that there were hard feelings toward Tycho that were put to rest only when the king intervened.'

The precise nature of that intervention is not known. However, Tycho's reputation as an astronomer continued to grow until at last, on May 23rd, 1576, spurred by a threat from Tycho that he would take himself off to Germany and ally himself to some prince there, King Frederick II put his signature to a document granting 'to our beloved Tycho Brahe . . . our land of Hven, with all our and the crown's tenants and servants who live thereon, and with all the rent and duty which comes from it . . . to have, enjoy, use, and hold; free, clear, without any rent, all the days of his life.' An offer, one would think, the Dane could not refuse. He hesitated nevertheless, canvassing friends and colleagues for their advice. They, at least, knew a good thing when they saw it. One of Tycho's old pals, the physician Johannes Pratensis, summed up the general feeling when he wrote of the King's offer: 'Apollo desires it, Urania recommends it, Mercury commands it with his staff.' For a watcher of the heavens such as Tycho, there is no disobeying the gods.

Still, he was not going to be rushed. He spent some months investigating his new domain, even measuring the island's circumference by pacing out the entire coast, finding it to be 8,160 strides in length. He seems to have put the fear of God into the locals, too, huddling in their thatched cottages in the only village on the island, Tuna, or on Hven's few scattered farms. From the start he had a bad reputation among the people for cruelty, arrogance and greed. As Kitty Ferguson puts it in *The Nobleman and His Housedog*, Tycho 'would come to seem, to the villagers of Hven and the descendants to whom they passed on the stories about him, not the enlightened genius of the age but a figure as mysterious and malign as the ancient Lady Grimmel herself.'

For generations the islanders had been virtually self-governing, and did not welcome the advent of this new lord. Straight off he got on their wrong side by choosing for the site of his observatory a large tract of land at the centre of the island that until then had been common grazing ground. This high-handedness was hardly in the spirit of King Frederick's document of grant, which had enjoined Tycho to 'observe the law and due right towards the peasants living there, and do them no injustice against the law, nor burden them with any new dues or uncustomary innovations.'

If ever there was an uncustomary innovation, surely it was Uraniborg, the palatial edifice that Tycho built to house his observatory, alchemical laboratory, residence and administrative centre. He designed it according to the ideas of Vitruvius and Palladio, following especially the latter's strictures on the harmonic proportioning of the individual parts of the building and of the parts to the whole. The result, as can be seen from contemporary woodcuts, was a cross between Frankenstein's castle and a giant gazebo. For twenty years Tycho would work here, building vast astronomical instruments which he used to map the sky with a thoroughness and accuracy undreamed of by anyone except him, and making Uraniborg the wonder of scientific Europe. But even wonders fade. Tycho's patron, King Frederick, died, and his successor, Christian, was far less indulgent. Uraniborg, and Tycho's increasingly grandiose projects there, were a drain upon the royal coffers. Pressure was brought to bear on Tycho; there were lawsuits, investigations were ordered by the Crown, he was accused of mistreating the peasants; on top of all this, the issue of his twenty-five-year morganatic marriage was raised again, and there was even a question as to the legitimacy of his children. Heartbreaking though it must have been for him, it was time to move on. In June of 1597, Tycho and his two-dozen-strong household took ship for Germany.

There followed eighteen months of uncertainty and worry for Tycho and his numerous dependants. During that time Tycho expended much energy in trying to get back into King Christian's favour, but without success. In the end, despairing of his homeland, Tycho turned his attention to Prague, that imperial city at the geographical and political centre of Europe. He knew of the Emperor Rudolf's interest in science and the occult arts, and had been in contact with a number of Rudolf's courtiers and advisers. At last, in the summer of 1599, the imperial summons came, and Tycho and his retinue set off southwards, the Brahe family riding in a splendid new coach purchased in Hamburg. All seemed set fair, and Tycho was filled with hope and a new sense of purpose. However, there was an ominous occurrence when, during an overnight halt at a castle along the way, Tycho's pet elk found its way to an upper floor, drank a dish of beer, and in the resulting inebriated state fell downstairs and broke its neck. Tycho was inconsolable at the loss of his beloved animal, perhaps seeing in its demise, as Rudolf saw in the death of his African lion, a dark portent of the future. Like most people of the time, even the educated ones, Tycho had his superstitions – he was, according to Gassendi, mortally afraid of rabbits and, inconveniently, old ladies – and no doubt the elk's death gave him a premonitory shiver.

Yet his reception in Prague was all he could have hoped for. When he arrived at the beginning of July he probably lodged at The Golden Griffin inn[23] on Nový Svĕt ('New World' Street)

[23] The inn no longer exists, but the first house on the street is called The Golden Griffin. Next door is The Golden Pear restaurant – also on Nový Svĕt are The Golden Lamb and The Golden Tree. The Golden Griffin house bears an interesting inscription (in Czech): 'In the year of our Lord MDCCCI a memorial plaque in honour of the famous Dane Tycho Brahe, imperial mathematician and astrologer, was erected at the expense of the municipality of Prague on this house, known of old as *U zlatého noha* (The Golden Griffin). Brahe

beside the castle grounds on the Hradčany and within easy distance of the Emperor's palace. However, the aristocratic Tycho would not stop long at a mere inn – besides, the tolling of bells from the nearby Capuchin monastery gave him a constant headache – and he made it plain that his prime requirement was an establishment of his own that would be spacious enough to accommodate his collection of mighty instruments, still on its way from Hven. On his first day in the city he was greeted, in one of the palace gardens, by Rudolf's private secretary, Johannes Barwitz, who welcomed him warmly and spoke of the Emperor's high regard for him. A few days afterwards he had his first audience with Rudolf himself. Tycho described the triumphal occasion to his disreputable cousin Frederick Rosenkrantz[24] in a letter which itself fairly swells with pride. In what indeed must have been an indication of special favour, Rudolf received him in private, 'sitting in the room on a bench with his

resided in this house in the year MDC and on 24th October MDCI died in a house which stood on the site of what is now the Černín Palace.' Enquiries at The Golden Pear were met with a denial that The Golden Griffin next door had ever been an inn, but someone seemed to remember that there had once been a restaurant of that name down on Nerudova Street. Everything shifts, in magic Prague.
[24] In 1592, this Rosenkrantz, along with another Brahe cousin, Knud Gyldenstierne, travelled on a diplomatic mission to London, where they must surely have encountered one of the leading English dramatists of the day . . .

back against a table, completely alone . . . without even an attending page.' That the Emperor was alone might have been boasted of as an indication of special favour, but Tycho the Meticulous found it necessary to point out that the absence from the royal chamber of the usual clutter of courtiers, petitioners and sentries might have been due to the fact that there was plague in the city, that some of the castle staff were thought to have been infected, and that Rudolf, as we already know, was a full-blown hypochondriac. Tycho made a speech in Latin, presented letters of introduction from the Bishop of Cologne and the Duke of Mecklenburg, which Rudolf graciously did not bother to read, 'and immediately responded to me graciously with a more detailed speech than the one I had delivered to him, saying, among other things, how agreeable my arrival was for him and that he promised to support me and my research, all the while smiling in the most kindly way so that his whole face beamed with benevolence.' The old boy must have been in a good mood that day. The moment comes to less than thunderous life in the letter's next sentence: 'I could not take in everything he said because he naturally speaks very softly.' One pictures them there, in sweltering midsummer, in that murmurous room, the seated Emperor, moist-eyed, pendulous of jaw, and the big, eager, blond Dane with his ruff and his moustache and his metal nose glinting.

When the audience was at an end and Tycho had stepped out of the room, secretary Barwitz was summoned inside for a word with the Emperor. He returned to tell Tycho that His Majesty, who obviously did not miss a thing, had looked down from his window and had seen him arriving at the castle, and, ever the beady-eyed collector, had wondered what was the mechanical device attached to his carriage. It seems this was a milometer, of Tycho's own making. Tycho had his son fetch the thing, and Barwitz brought it into the Emperor's chamber, returning after a little while to say that His Majesty had one or two such devices already – well, he would have, of course – but not so large or made in the same way. Tycho hastened to offer his as a gift, but Rudolf said he would content himself by having one of his craftsmen construct a similar one based on Tycho's design. Barwitz also assured Tycho again of the Emperor's high regard for him, and his determination to confer him with an annual grant and to provide suitable quarters for him and his family. Tycho was delighted; here at last was a royal who knew how to treat a man of genius.

Despite his capriciousness and extreme prone-ness to suspicion, Rudolf was indeed a remarkably steadfast patron. He stuck doggedly by his magi-cians and necromancers – what is the collective noun: an alembic of alchemists, an abyss of alche-mists? – despite their inevitable failure to locate the philosopher's stone or distil the elixir of life. Repeated disappointments and even betrayals could not destroy his faith in the power and efficacy of magic. When the great Doctor John Dee, 'who understood the language of the birds and could speak the idiom of Adam the proto-plast', as Ripellino tells us, arrived in Prague in 1584 he brought with him the infamous Edward Kelley, who among other unlikelihoods boasted of being able to conjure spirits in Dee's magic mirror, a sphere of smoky quartz the Doctor claimed had been given him by the angel Uriel. Kelley was an Irishman, or at least was of Irish descent, officially but somewhat confusedly de-scribed in the Sněmy České (national records of the Czech legislative assembly, the Sněm), as 'Eduard Kelley, born an Englishman, of the knightly kin and house called Imaymi in the county of Conaghaku in the kingdom of Ireland' Kelley was known to Praguers as a *Jahrmarkts-doktor*, or mountebank, and, even less flatter-ingly, a *cacochymicus*, which does not require translation. His real name was Talbot, and he was born not in the 'country of Conaghaku' (Connaught?) but in Worcester. In 1580 he was arrested for forgery and as punishment had his ears cut off by the Lancaster executioner. Earlessness, added to his hooked nose and pinkish eyes, gave him a decidedly, and no doubt useful, aspect of the diabolical. In his wanderings about England he had discovered in a Welsh pub, so he swore, a magical document which had come from the grave of a magician, along with two phials, containing respectively a red and a white powder. The document was written in an indecipherable language, but Kelley was convinced it contained the formula for the philosopher's stone. He brought parchment and phials to Dee's laboratory at Mortlake in London, and was appointed the great man's assistant. Doctor Dee, it seems, was as gullible as his future royal patron. But then, Dee himself had claimed to have found some of the elixir of life in the ruins of Glastonbury.[25]

On a visit to England in 1583, the Palatine of

---

[25] Yet Dee should not be underestimated, or regarded in the same light as Kelley. In his book *Rudolf II and His World*, R.J.W. Evans, drawing on a number of scholarly studies as well as his own research, takes Dee very seriously indeed. 'Dee's broad metaphysical position,' Evans writes, 'was characteristic of an intellectual of his time: he believed in the theory of the microcosm, in hidden forces underlying the visible world, in cosmic harmony. His views led him . . . to advanced astronomical speculations. At the same time he

Sieradz, Olbracht Łaski, a great Catholic land-
owner, visited Dee at Mortlake, where a spirit
appeared in Dee's crystal ball and predicted that
Łaski would inherit the Polish throne. The thrilled
and grateful Łaski promptly invited Dee and his
assistant to come to Poland, and it was from
Cracow, perhaps hurrying away from another
disappointed patron – Łaski never did get to wear
crown of Poland – that the pair arrived in Prague
only a year after Rudolf had transferred his court
there from Vienna in 1583. Dee, whose fame as
Elizabeth of England's chief sorcerer had gone
before him, was welcomed by Rudolf – Dee had
visited Rudolf's father, Maximilian, twenty years
before, and dedicated one of his most important
works, the *Monas Hieroglyphia*, to him – and
proceeded at once to bamboozle the Emperor by
pretending to transmogrify mercury into gold,
and conjuring, with Kelley's help, a host of spirits
in his crystal mirror. This seems to have been the

believed . . . that access to these mysteries could be achieved
through such things as symbols, intellectual 'keys', and combinations . . . [T]here is no doubt that Dee felt the spirit world to be a full
reality. Whatever the origin of the messages which it communicated
to him, Dee believed them unwaveringly, and when set against the
contemporary mood of intellectual striving the schemes of universal
reform and regeneration which he derived from his seances grow
much more comprehensible.' (*Rudolf II and His World*, p. 219)
Evans is an indulgent judge, and makes a case even for Kelley,
noting the high esteem in which he was held by many of his
contemporaries, not all of them fools.

only time Dee was able to speak directly to the Emperor. The Catholic party in Prague was highly suspicious of this English magician, a favourite of the anathematised Queen Elizabeth, after all, and a Protestant, or so they thought – in fact, Dee held to a chiliastic form of universal Christianity unfettered by dogma. By 1586, two years after his arrival in Prague, Dee was being accused by the Papal Nuncio of having dealings with the Devil, and Rudolf had no choice but to banish him, ordering him to be gone within a day; Dee remained in the area, however, under the protection of the rich nobleman Vilém of Rožmberk on his estate at Třeboň, returning to England in 1594. Unadvisedly, Rudolf set Kelley in Dee's place.

Kelley did very well for himself in the Emperor's service, earning enough gold to buy a brewery and a mill and a number of houses in the city – one of them, according to legend, the house in the sinister Cattle Market, now Charles Square, in which Dr Faust lived; the Faustův Dům, or Faust House, still stands at Karlovo náměstí 40.[26] Fortuna, however, is a fickle mistress, and after his time at the top

[26] In *Magic Prague* Ripellino is fascinating on the subject of Faust: 'According to legend, which made the Czech Romantics swell with pride, Faust was a Czech who practised the black arts, that is, necromancy and printing. His name was Šťastný, that is, Happy, that is, Faustus. During the Hussite Revolt he emigrated to Germany, where he took the name Faust von Kuttenberg after the town of his birth (Kutna Horá in Czech). In other words, he was none

Kelley's subsequent turns of the wheel were all downward. In 1591 he killed one of Rudolf's courtiers in a duel, and although he lost no time in going on the run, the Emperor's police caught up with him, and after another sword fight he was imprisoned at Křivoklát Castle. He remained there for two and a half years, then one night, having bribed the jailer, he lowered himself from the window of his cell on a rope. However, the rope broke and he fell into the moat, where he was found next morning, unconscious and with a broken leg. Rudolf relented and allowed him to return to Prague, where his leg, by now infected, had to be amputated and replaced with a wooden one. So now the earless sorcerer was also a pegleg. By now he had run out of property and money, his Bohemian wife had to pawn her jewellery, and eventually Rudolf had the bankrupt thrown into prison again, this time at Most Castle, eighty kilometres upriver from Prague, from where even the diplomatic intervention of Sir William Cecil, Queen Elizabeth's Secretary of State, could not rescue him. Never daunted, Kelley attempted the

other than Gutenberg, the inventor of the printing press . . . In Czech folk puppet plays, the *pimprlata* theatre, Faust is the more conventional figure of the *Faustbücher* even if, when conjuring up 'Alexander the Great with the cloak of a Czech duke and the fair Helen in Turkish dress' at the court in Lisbon, he comes dangerously close to the Czech Punch – Kašpárek by name – who mistakes devils for owls.' (*Magic Prague*, p. 97)

John Banville

rope trick again, but again the rope broke and he fell once more into the moat, smashing his remaining leg. Hauled back to his cell, he took his own life by drinking a phial of poison smuggled to him by his wife, who perhaps was, understandably, impatient for her viduity. Kelley died on November 1st, 1597.[27]

[27] Kelley was not the worst, and not even the most extravagant, of the mountebanks to take advantage of Rudolf's, and Prague's, gullibility. There was Mamugna of Famagosta, a Greek masquerading as the son of the Venetian Marco Antonio Bragadin, who had been flayed alive by the Turks during the siege of Famagusta. Mamugna arrived in Prague during Kelley's reign, accompanied by two enormous, black, satanic mastiffs. He had a brief success in the city, winkling much gold out of the Prague grandees. In 1591 he was unmasked as an imposter and fled to Munich, but found no sanctuary there, for he was hanged on a gilt gallows and buried in a pauper's grave along with the carcasses of his dogs. The Italian adventurer Geronimo Scotta appeared in Prague in the summer of 1590 with no fewer than three red velvet carriages drawn by forty horses. He was a skilled conman, whose speciality was contracting rich marriages and then absconding with the dowries. He quickly found his way into Rudolf's favour, but Kelley, who could spot a fellow rogue a mile off, soon proved his undoing, and Scotta ended up selling stag-horn jelly and vitriol of Mars from a booth in the Old Town Square. (Evans, in his book on Rudolfine Prague, speculates that in fact Kelley and Scotta, or Scotto, may have been one and the same person.) None of these crooks, however, was as outrageous as Michael Sendivogius, a Polish sorcerer, and his henchman, the mysterious Alexander Seton, a Scot known as the Cosmopolitan, who performed magic spells with the aid of an unidentified red powder. The pair are too much larger than life to be dealt with in a mere footnote. (Ripellino is splendidly entertaining on the scores of rogues who plagued the credulous Rudolf.) Seton died in Dresden after Sendivogius had sprung him from imprisonment at Königstein Castle, where he had been tortured in a vain effort to make him reveal the formula for his magic red powder. Sendivogius himself was hanged in Stuttgart, like Mamugna on a gilt gallows, magnificently dressed in a gold-sequined suit.

Rudolf surely suffered a tremor of foreboding when, not long after Kelley's demise, he found himself confronted by yet another outlandish foreigner with a prosthesis. Big blond Tycho of the flowing moustache and metal nose must have seemed a very Viking to the pyknik Emperor. All the more remarkable then that Brahe should have been received at the imperial court with such warmth and generosity. Of course, the Dane had a Europe-wide reputation as an astronomer, but Kelley had been vouched for by Doctor Dee who in turn had been favoured by Elizabeth I.[28] Nevertheless, Rudolf was as good as his promise of patronage, and offered to settle Tycho and his extended family in the house of the former pro-chancellor Jacob Kurtz – Kurtz was dead – which Tycho described as 'a splendid and magnificent palace (which [Kurtz] had built in the Italian style, with beautiful private grounds, at a cost of more than 20,000 dalers).' The house stood

[28] Rumours have persisted down the ages, entertained by Ripellino and others but discounted by such authorities as Evans and Frances Yates, that Dee and Kelley were agents sent to Prague by Elizabeth or her wily Chief Secretary Sir William Cecil to seek Bohemian help in England's struggles with Spain, or else to work at preventing a Habsburg seizure of the Polish crown. Ripellino the romantic rubs his hands, of course, at the notion that the two might have been spies – 'spooks' is here the *mot juste* – declaring that 'it would mean that the whole business of mirrors, omens and archangels was simply a camouflage for political intrigues and the diary in which Dee recorded his conversations with the heavenly messengers a cover or memorandum in code.'

on the brow of Hradčany hill to the west of the palace; it is no longer there, but gigantic statues of Tycho and Kepler have been erected on the site, near the Černín Palace. Secretary Barwitz showed the Dane over the property, but Tycho was not satisfied, noting that the tower attached to the house would not be large enough to accommodate even one of the astronomical instruments he had brought with him from Hven. Barwitz, no doubt accustomed to the lordly caprices of Rudolf's clients, suggested that perhaps Herr Brahe would prefer to have one of the outlying imperial castles. The choice seems to have been between the Emperor's favourite hunting lodge, Brandýs, and a property perched on a hill some forty kilometres or a six-hour carriage ride from the city. Benátky Castle stood in beautiful surroundings above the floodplain of the river Jizera, and was known as 'Bohemian Venice' because when the river was in spate the country round about was under water. Tycho was delighted. At the landlocked heart of Europe, here was another Hven. Before the end of August, the Brahes had moved into Benátky, and Tycho had set up his first instrument.[29]

---

[29] Benátky Castle has been turned into a small, not very well appointed museum, run by an extremely charming and helpful staff. When I visited the place in the 1990s I was the only visitor. I stood in the echoing rooms trying to feel the lingering presence of the Dane, but no ghosts walked, that day.

At once, Tycho embarked on a lavish rebuilding programme at the Emperor's expense. Within weeks the administrator of the estate, Caspar von Mühlstein, was sending urgent warnings to Barwitz about the mounting cost of the Dane's renovations. It was the beginning of a series of wranglings with imperial officials that would continue to Tycho's death and beyond. To complicate matters, a month after Tycho's move to Benátky there was yet another outbreak of plague in the city and the Emperor had fled the Hradčany for the safety of the countryside. Inevitably the plague reached Benátky, and when the death toll in the area had reached 2,000 Tycho himself – urged, as he loftily pointed out, by his womenfolk, who were frightened – he temporarily abandoned the nascent new Uraniborg and retreated thirty kilometers downriver to a castle at Girsitz. He was still there when, at the beginning of 1600, Johannes Kepler arrived in Prague, and thus there was a delay to one of the most momentous meetings in the history of science.

It would be hard to imagine two more dissimilar figures than Kepler and Tycho Brahe. Kepler, the younger of the two by twenty-five years, was born in 1571 – at 2.30 pm on December 27th of that year, to be precise, which Kepler liked to be – on the northern fringes of the Black Forest, in the town of Weilderstadt, a 'free city' within the duchy of Württemberg. The family were a mixed lot; Grandfather Sebald was for a time Bürghermeister of Weilderstadt, while his son Sebaldus was, in Johannes Kepler's laconic description of him, 'an astrologer, a Jesuit, acquired a wife, caught the French sickness, was vicious.' Kepler's father, a professional mercenary, was a braggart and a bully who cruelly mistreated his wife and children, eventually abandoning them altogether to go off to the Low Countries to fight with the Duke of Alba's marauders. The mother, Katarina, was quick-witted but cold; like her son, she was fascinated by the natural world, although her interest in herbs and homemade medicines would eventually lead to her being tried on a charge of witchcraft. Johannes was a sickly child, made sicklier by being sent out to work as a farm labourer at the age of eight. Eventually he was put back to school, and received an excellent education thanks to the enlightened policies of the Duke of Württemberg. At seventeen he entered the University of Tübingen, where he was taught by the famous Michael Mästlin, a mathematician and astronomer admired even by the great Tycho Brahe.

Kepler was both a devout Protestant and a

follower of Pythagoras – the philosopher of the fifth century BC who taught that the universe is centred not on the Earth but on an eternal, invisible flame – and held to the revolutionary theory of Copernicus, who had set the sun at the focus of planetary motion. These were daring beliefs for a young man to hold in those times of religious upheaval and repression.[30] He also read widely in the work of the Neoplatonists, and of the mystic and philosopher Cardinal Nicholas of Cusa, who had anticipated Copernicus by a century by declaring that the Earth does not stand still at the centre of the world. From Tübingen in his third year Kepler was directed by the university authorities to take up the post of schoolteacher in Graz in southern Austria. Kepler was aghast at the prospect of being buried alive in the far-off and backward province of Styria; even to get there he would lose ten days because of the different calendar in use in Graz. Nevertheless he bowed to authority, and took up his post at the seminary school in 1594, at the age of twenty-two. His subjects were advanced mathematics, including astronomy. He was a terrible teacher: in his first year he had a handful of students, in his second, none. He also held the position of

[30] Giordano Bruno was burned at the stake for preaching the Copernican doctrine.

District Mathematician, which, despite the high sound of it, meant he would be required chiefly to draw up astrological predictions for the town and district at the beginning of each new year. Kepler maintained an ambivalent attitude to astrology, the 'foolish little daughter' of astronomy, as he called it, yet throughout his life he continued to cast horoscopes for himself and his family, especially his children. He took great care with these star charts, while being not at all averse to massaging the data in order to avoid unfavourable predictions.

Kepler recorded the moment, on July 19th, 1595, when his life as a scientist may be said truly to have begun. He was in the classroom of the Graz seminary school, conducting a lesson in astronomy. He had drawn on the blackboard a diagram illustrating the progression of the great conjunctions of Jupiter and Saturn, that is, the crossing points at which, approximately every twenty years, the planet Jupiter catches up with and passes Saturn. Because of slight variations in distance between the points on the Zodiac at which the conjunctions occur – pay attention, please, this is really not as complicated as it seems – it is possible to inscribe a series of triangles within the circle of the Zodiac joining the conjunction points, triangles which on their inner sides will, as if by magic, or divine intention, 'draw' another, smaller circle . . . Oh, all right, here is an illustration.

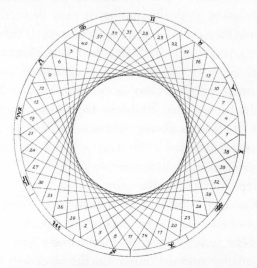

For years already Kepler the astronomer had been pondering essential questions, such as why there should be six planets – only six were known in his day – and why the distances between their orbits should be set as they are. There must be a plan, a rational design; as Einstein centuries later would insist, God does not play dice with the world.[31] To Kepler the Pythagorean, the planetary system was a gigantic musical instrument sounding its vast,

---

[31] According to quantum physics, He does.

silent chord in tune to the geometric laws of harmony. It was a conviction he shared with most astronomers back to antiquity. Kepler's genius, his astonishing originality, lay in the way he tackled the questions that he never stopped asking. Before him, cosmologists had bent their best efforts to describing the disposition of things as they seemed, and predicting accurately how things might be expected to be in the future. Kepler was the first to concentrate not on description, but explanation. He wanted to know not only how things are as they are, but why. A plan, a pattern, there must be.

That day in the schoolroom in Graz when he stepped back from the blackboard – let us imagine the summer sunlight in the dusty window, the chalk-motes drifting in the luminous air, the bored pupils drooping at their desks, one of them dreamily picking his nose – what Kepler saw was that the inner circle was half the size of the outer one. Saturn and Jupiter were the two outermost planets of the solar system, as it was known to him, and Jupiter's orbit was roughly half the size of Saturn's. Was the relationship between them dictated by a triangle, the first figure in geometry? And if so, could the relations between the orbits of the remaining planets also be set according to the dimensions of other geometrical forms? He spent the rest of the summer trying to discover what these forms might be, juggling triangles and squares and pentagons, like Beckett's Molloy shuffling his sucking stones from pocket to pocket. And at last it came to him, when he saw that of course he must move from two to three dimensions. In geometry there are five, and only five, regular or perfect solids, from the cube, with six identical sides, up to the icosahedron, which has twenty sides. It is a characteristic of these shapes that they can be set within a sphere so that all their corners touch the surface of the sphere, and that a sphere can be set inside them so that the

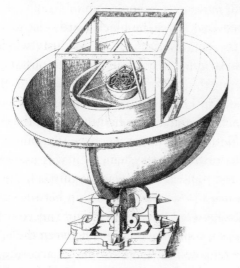

Kepler's model of the universe, from *Mysterium Cosmograpicum*

surface of the sphere will touch the centre of every side. Perfection. This was it, Kepler believed, God's big secret, the framework of the planetary system, the grid of the great world. This was why there are, as he thought, six planets, because the Lord of the Universe had founded the solar system on the five perfect solids, one set inside each of the planetary orbits, with the sun at the centre.

Kepler was to devote the rest of his life to proving his theory, despite the fact that it was unprovable, because mistaken. Even after he had made the momentous discovery that the planets do not move in perfect circles, but in ellipses, and had devised his three laws of planetary motion which revolutionised astronomy and the science of physics, he still clung to his beautiful idea, resorting to some shameless mathematical sleight of hand in his efforts to smooth out the inconsistencies. In the summer of 1595, however, in the first flush of discovery, his immediate need was for the most accurate planetary observations then available. He thought at once of Tycho Brahe. However, it would be more than four years before he would meet the Dane, and even then it took another year and a half, and Tycho's death, for this 'little house dog', as he liked to describe himself, to get his teeth into the juicy meat of Tycho's planetary charts. By then he was a married man with a stepdaughter – his wife, Barbara, twenty-three when he met her, was already twice a widow – and the author of a book setting out his theory of the heavens, with the catchy title *Prodromus dissertationum cosmographicarum, continens mysterium cosmographicum, de admirabili proportione orbium coelestium, deque causis coelorum numeri, magnitudinis, motuumque periodicorum genuinis & proprijis, demonstratum, per quinque regularia corpora geometrica,* or *Mysterium cosmographicum* for short.

In the final years of the sixteenth century life had become extremely difficult for Protestants in the province of Styria. The Counter-Reformation was well under way, and the Catholic authorities in Graz were imposing increasingly harsh religious strictures. When in the summer of 1599 the Keplers' baby daughter Susanna died after less than a month of life, Kepler refused a Catholic burial for the infant and was consequently fined. In the autumn, rumours began to fly that soon any Lutheran moving out of the city would have his wealth and possessions confiscated, which, if the rumours were true, would mean that the Keplers would lose Barbara's considerable inheritance. There were sectarian riots in the countryside, and then in the streets of the city itself. The time had come to move on. Kepler turned his increasingly desperate attention in the direction of Prague. Tycho Brahe, the Great Dane in the manger, possessed a wealth of astronomical data. 'Only, like most rich men,' Kepler wrote to his old teacher Mästlin, 'he does not know how to make proper use of his riches. Therefore, one must take pains to wring his treasures from him, to get from him, by begging, the decision to publish all his observations without reservation.' Later, in 1601, Kepler wrote from Prague to the Italian astronomer Antonio Magini of his reasons for coming there: 'What influenced me most was the hope of completing my study of the harmony of the world – something that I have long contemplated and that I would be able to complete only if Tycho were to rebuild astronomy or if I could use his observations.' Despite his double vision, Kepler was never less than clear-eyed.

At the beginning of 1600 Kepler's chance came. An acquaintance of his, Baron Johann Friedrich Hoffmann, a wealthy, cultured man and a close adviser to the Emperor Rudolf, had been in Graz to attend a convention of the Styrian Diet and was now returning to Prague, and offered him a lift in his entourage. The Baron was of a kindly disposition, and, although a Catholic, had sympathy with Kepler's difficulties as a Lutheran. Also, Hoffmann was an amateur astronomer, and had read and admired Kepler's work. He was acquainted too with Tycho Brahe and had determined that the two men should meet. And Kepler did need a friendly advocate, for he had already blundered into a series of embarrassing and potentially disastrous misunderstandings with the prickly Dane, including seeming to back up the claims of a certain Nicholaus Reymers Bär – his punningly Latinised name was Ursus, *ursus* being Latin for bear – who had briefly assisted Tycho on Hven, and had published a system of the world which Tycho vehemently claimed was a plagiarism of his own work; Tycho would have got in first, were it not for his extreme unwillingness to publish, since in his circle and among his family the writing of books was considered no fit occupation for a gentleman and a knight. However, Tycho in his lordly way had forgiven young Kepler his trespasses, and had written graciously to invite him to Prague, assuring him that 'whatever comes to pass, you will find in me not a follower of fortune . . . but your friend who even under untoward circumstances will not fail you with his advice and help, but rather will advance you to everything that is best,' Kepler, however, did not receive this letter, for it crossed with his journey to Prague.

Arriving in the city in the bitterly cold dawn of a new century – it was January, 1600 – Kepler, no doubt exhausted after the ten-day journey, was alarmed to find that Brahe, like Old Possum's cat Macavity, was not there. He was not even at Benátky, for he was still sheltering from the plague at Girsitz. Kepler, who had left Barbara and her seven-year-old daughter Regina in Graz, lodged with the hospitable Baron Hoffmann at his house on the Hradčany, in a street behind the royal gardens that would one day be called Tychonova, named after you know who. What an adventure Prague must have been for this poor son of Weilderstadt. The transfer of the imperial court from Vienna had made Prague the first city of the empire, and for the thirty years of Rudolf's rule there it was the centre of Europe not only geographically but in terms of wealth and power. Like every capital city it acted as a magnet, drawing to it people from all over the continent, ambassadors and foreign diplomats, scholars, artists, scores of alchemists and sorcerers and, inevitably, as we have seen, countless mountebanks and swindlers. To Kepler the city must have been a dazzling spectacle, a very image of the 'gold rooms and spontaneous applause, the attention of magnificent people'[32] that he had anticipated. There were magnificent Gothic palaces and Romanesque churches,[33] while the Castle itself, brooding on its hill, must have seemed a city within a city. Kepler will have cast a speculative eye toward the Hradčany, Rudolf's keep, for he knew of the Emperor's enthusiasm for new science and old magic, in the first of which Kepler was an adept, and the second of which he was prepared to practise, if horoscopes and numerology should prove the route into imperial favour.

At the end of January, when the cold had killed off the last of the pestilence, Tycho returned to Benátky, and wrote another letter to Kepler. This one got delivered. In it, Tycho was promisingly cordial, inviting Kepler to the Bohemian Venice, the new Uraniborg. 'You will come,' the Dane wrote, 'not so much as guest but as a very welcome friend and highly desirable participant and companion in our observations of the

[32] Ahem. John Banville, *Kepler*, a novel (London, 1981).
[33] The finest Romanesque survival is the Basilica of St George, after St Vitus's the largest church within the Castle complex. The Cistercians arrived there in the 13th century and brought a French influence to the city's architecture, still to be seen in St Agnes's Convent, founded by the sister of Wenceslas I, on U milosrdných in Josefov, the old Jewish Quarter. It was abolished as a convent in 1782, but was restored in the 1960s and now houses a collection of nineteenth-century Czech art from the National Gallery. Don't say I do not give practical advice.

heavens.' In a further show of favour he sent his son, Tycho the younger, accompanied by Franz Tengnagel, an elegant young Westphalian noble and one of the astronomer's assistants, to Prague to fetch the newcomer. When Kepler and his two escorts reached Benátky, Tycho received him warmly, offering to reimburse his travel expenses and enquiring after his family and what plans he had for his wife and stepdaughter to join him. Kepler could scarcely contain his excitement and joy. The world's greatest, or at least its most renowned, astronomer – Kepler had no doubt who the really great one was – the legendary lord of Hven, magus of Uraniborg, and now Imperial Mathematician to His Majesty Rudolf II, was shaking his hand and inviting him to join with him in work to solve the *mysterium cosmographicum.*

Within a day or two, however, Kepler's hopes had turned to ashes. He had not yet learned the ways of the aristocracy, and had mistaken Tycho's automatically courtly greeting for a pledge of comradeship. When the niceties were done with, Tycho promptly turned and swept away to his own concerns, which were many and burdensome. Benátky was still a building site, with workmen traipsing everywhere, hammering and whistling. Four of Brahe's most precious instruments were still on Hven, while others were in transit somewhere in the German lands. And Kepler was not the only one being disappointed in the matter of patronage: the Emperor's pledges of financial support for Tycho and his plans had not been made good, while Mühlstein, the increasingly alarmed administrator of Benátky, was refusing to countenance further expenditure on renovations to the castle without direct authorisation from the Emperor.

Life for the exiles at Benátky was chaotic, noisy, crowded and yet isolated, 'a reigning loneliness of people,' in Kepler's mournfully poetic description – the Brahes, after all, were farther away from home than he was. Mealtimes on the upper floor of the castle were a torment for Kepler, a ceaseless din of raucous Danish talk and the clatter of crockery and wine mugs. Lord Brahe presided gloomily at the head of the table, his dwarf jester Jeppe squatting cross-legged at his feet, while his wife and their daughters squabbled and shrieked, and the numerous attendants and scientific assistants gossiped endlessly while jostling for placement above the salt. Hogsheads of wine were swilled down, so that the normally abstemious Kepler must have spent the first weeks of his stay in a more or less permanent semi-stupor. The access to astronomical treasures that Tycho had promised him was not forthcoming. Tycho himself was not forthcoming. In the course of dinner Kepler would wheedle his way up the table to where the great man sat, ignoring him except on the rare occasions when he deigned to let fall, like a scrap from his plate, a bit of information on the orbit of Mars, or lunar occlusions, or coming conjunctions between this or that of the planets. Where was that 'companionship in our observations' that Tycho had so enticingly offered? Instead of the equal in scientific knowledge that Tycho had seemed to consider him, he was, he realised, no more to the Dane than a *domesticus*, a hired man. What he did not realise was the extent of Tycho's wariness and sense of foreboding. Although Kepler was not yet the scientist that he would be in later years, he was, Tycho knew, a formidable rival in the race for immortality. One of the strong reasons for Tycho's unwillingness to give up his precious astronomical data to this young man half his age was the fear that Kepler the Copernican would use them to prove that Copernicus's sun-centred system was correct. For Tycho had his own system, a not inelegant one but, as Kepler would indeed prove, no more than a hopelessly mistaken compromise between Ptolemy's ancient geocentric model and the heliocentric version proposed by Copernicus.

In the weeks and months that followed, the little dog which Kepler had once compared himself to turned snappish, and on occasion even vicious.[34] Grudgingly, Tycho had opened the coffers of his accumulated observations and given him the orbit of Mars to work on. Careful as always, however, he placed Kepler under the supervision of another Tychonic assistant, Christian Sorensen, called Longomontanus after the Danish village of Longberg where he was born – how they did love those Latinate puns! – a mild, well-meaning man whose authority over him Kepler deeply though silently resented. Yet the two men worked well together, thanks mainly to Longomontanus's tolerance and unmistakable brilliance as an astronomer. In time, Tycho

[34] At the age of twenty-six Kepler had written this half-serious, third-person description of himself: 'That man has in every way a dog-like nature. His appearance is that of a little house dog. His body is agile, wiry, and well-proportioned. Even his appetites were the same: he liked gnawing bones and dry crusts of bread, and was so greedy that whatever his eyes chanced on he grabbed; yet, like a dog, he drinks little and is content with the simplest food. His habits also were like those of a house dog . . . He was constantly on the move, digging among the sciences, politics, and private affairs, even the most trivial kind; always following someone else, imitating his thoughts and actions. He is impatient with conversation but greets visitors just like a dog; yet when the smallest thing is snatched away from him he flares up and growls. He tenaciously persecutes wrong-doers – that is, he barks at them. He is malicious and bites people with his sarcasms. He hates many people exceedingly and they avoid him, but his masters are fond of him. He has a dog-like horror of baths, tinctures and lotions.'

relaxed enough to reassign Longomontanus to lunar theory – the moon was an important player in the drama of the Tychonic system – and allow Kepler to continue to work on Mars alone, but not before he had compelled Kepler to sign a pledge not to reveal any of the secrets of the new Uraniborg to the outside world. The assignment of the Mars project to Kepler was one of history's luckier chances, since the eccentricities of that planet's orbit could only be accounted for in relation to the position of the sun, a fact which supported Kepler's long-held theory that the sun is the source of planetary motion. Those weeks of work on Mars marked the maturing of Kepler's genius as a theoretical scientist.

Growing into his greatness, Kepler began to clamour for his rights. He demanded a contract from Tycho, one that would recognise him as an equal partner in the great cosmological project under way at Benátky, and guarantee him fitting recompense for his labours. Throughout that spring, negotiations between the two men dragged on. Kepler demanded that he be paid two separate salaries, one from Tycho and one from the Emperor, that he should have all afternoons free to work on his own theories, and that he and his family – Barbara and her daughter were still in Graz, anxiously awaiting the summons to Benátky – should be given a house to themselves, away from the castle and the disorderly life there. Not the least remarkable aspect of these discussions was the fact that while Kepler's hysteria and paranoia grew, Tycho displayed wholly uncharacteristic patience and forbearance. He was still suspicious of Kepler's Copernican leanings, but recognised, however unwillingly and with whatever foreboding, the young man's genius. It is possible too that beneath the aristocratic hauteur, Tycho simply liked his excitable, energetic and unintentionally comic collaborator. Certainly he indulged Kepler in ways that the other workers at Benátky would not have dared to dream of.

At the beginning of April, Tycho and Kepler sat down to thrash out an agreement, with the Emperor's chief physician, Jan Jesenský, acting as referee. Kepler had written to Tycho setting out his demands, and now Tycho produced a document in response, the main element of which was the secrecy pledge. If Kepler signed, Tycho would press the Emperor to grant Kepler a decent salary, would try to find a house for him and his family, and would pay travelling expenses for Barbara and her daughter to come from Graz. Kepler's demand for Sundays and holidays free Tycho regarded as an impertinence, insisting that he had never asked his assistants to work on those days. There was that word again: assistant. Kepler was adamant: either his demands must be met in full, or there would be no agreement. Despite Dr Jesenský's best emollient efforts the meeting broke up in rancour. At dinner that evening, in the presence of the Brahe household, Kepler got drunk on wine and launched a shrill attack on Tycho, who responded with equal energy. One imagines the scene, little Kepler, red with rage and too much alcohol, waving his fists and shrieking, while the Dane grips the edge of the table as if preparatory to upending it, the rumblings of his anger sounding like a ground bass under Kepler's frantic pipings. The following day, Kepler walked out, and returned to Prague in the company of Jesenský. Once again, Tycho displayed extraordinary restraint, although he did inform Jesenský before the two left that a written apology from Kepler would be required before he could return to Benátky and resume his work. It might be thought that this demand would send Kepler into greater heights of indignation and rage, but once back in Prague, staying probably at Baron Hoffmann's house, and no doubt urged to caution by Jesenský and the good Baron, he bethought himself and the perils of his position, and wrote a letter of apology to Tycho notable for its florid abjectness. The little dog had come to heel. Relieved, Tycho took the unprecedented step of summoning his carriage at once and riding into Prague in person to fetch the prodigal home to Benátky. Spring sunshine outside the Hoffmann house, and a humbled Kepler steps forth, blinking; alighting from his carriage the Dane sweeps forward, his metal nose agleam; a brocaded arm is thrown around drooping shoulders, gruff words are exchanged; the Baron and Dr Jesenský beam at each other over Kepler's head; the bells of St Vitus's begin to bang out a general rejoicing.

Back at Benátky, Tycho and Kepler quickly came to agreement on the latter's terms of employment. The Emperor would appoint Kepler as Tycho's assistant for a term of two years, during which time Kepler would continue to receive his salary as Styria's District Mathematician, along with a grant of half that amount again from the imperial purse. Arrangements were also put in place to fetch Kepler's wife and stepdaughter from Graz. In May Kepler travelled south to Styria, accompanied, at Tycho's direction, by the scapegrace Frederick Rosenkrantz, who was on his way to Vienna to join the Austrian army to fight against the Turks.[35] At last all seemed set fair for Kepler's life and work; as usual, everything went wrong. On June 10th, Rudolf returned to Prague from Plzeň, where he had gone nine months before to escape the plague. There was a backlog in the affairs of state, many decisions were called for, and the advice of the Imperial Mathematician – read: imperial astrologer – would be required on a daily, nay, an hourly basis. Tycho must come at once to Prague. Accommodation was arranged for him, his family and assistants at The Golden Griffin. Tycho, of course, was appalled. Work on Benátky was nearing completion, the northern shipping lanes had thawed sufficiently to allow the rest of his instruments to be sent down from Hven, and now, suddenly, he must abandon the New Uraniborg and be subject once more to the whims of an Emperor whose extreme eccentricities seemed to be tumbling over into plain madness. It was small comfort to the Dane when Rudolf expelled the Capuchins and their unbearable bells from their monastery behind The Golden Griffin; the good monks insisted Tycho was behind the expulsion, since the odour of sanctity which their prayers diffused about the Hradčany

---

[35] It is probably a good thing that they were not going to London, and that Gyldenstierne was not with them.

would surely be a hindrance to the dark and devilish works in which Brahe the well-known alchemist was no doubt engaged.[36] Tycho indeed had complained of the inadequacies of The Golden Griffin, so loudly that the Emperor quickly agreed to resettle him and his people in a house 'near Baron Hoffman's' on present-day Tychonova Street.[37] Rudolf further directed that Tycho might set up his astronomical instruments on the superb arcade of the very beautiful imperial summer palace, the so-called Belvedere.[38] These

[36] The Capuchins' pique is understandable, if only for the fact that Rudolf had taken a shine to their miraculous statue of the Madonna and Child and borrowed it to put in his private chapel at the palace. However, the statue promptly made its own way back to the monastery – one pictures the indignant Mother, golden babe in arms, striding indignantly home across the Hradčany at dead of night. Three times the statue was moved, and three times it returned. Impressed, the Emperor left the Lady and her Little One to the monks, and even presented the Virgin Mother with a gold crown and robe, which is perhaps what Mary had been angling for all along.

[37] There is some confusion among the biographies as to whether at this time Tycho moved into another house, perhaps on Tychonova, or back into the late Baron Kurtz's Italian-style palace on the west side of the Hradčany, where Tycho had lived when he first came to Prague. I am particularly struck by the mention of the Černín Palace on the plaque outside The Golden Griffin house on Nový Svět (see footnote 23 on page 143). This enormous pile was built in 1668 on the site where once stood the Kurtz house; if the plaque is right, and Tycho did die there, it must be that this is where he lived for those last months in Prague, and not on Tychonova.

[38] The Belvedere still stands, lovely and delicate among the massy edifices crowding the Hradčany. The *Blue Guide* describes it as 'one of the purest examples in central Europe of the Italian Renaissance style'. Chateaubriand admired it, on a visit to Prague in 1833, although he did worry about how cold the place would be in Prague's unitalianate winters.

facilities were not ideal, certainly not when compared with those at Benátky; when he had in-
stalled his instruments in the new premises – and
his library of three thousand books – Tycho
discovered to his dismay that a large part of
the sky in the southwest was obscured by the
buildings of the royal place. Still, he would have
to make do.

Meanwhile, in Graz, Kepler was floundering
in water that got hotter and hotter as the summer advanced. First of all the Styrian authorities
had refused to grant him leave to work in
Prague, then said they would not continue to
pay his salary as District Mathematician, despite
the Emperor's instructions – Protestant Styria
gave scant heed to the wishes of Rudolf the
Catholic. Kepler's hopes of working with Tycho
were waning, and in desperation he sought the
sponsorship of the Austrian Archduke, Ferdinand II. Ferdinand did not reply to Kepler's
beseechings; worse, at the end of July he issued
a decree expelling from the province all Protestants unwilling to convert to Catholicism. Kepler, whose increasingly radical scientific
theories served only to strengthen his Lutheran
faith, would not contemplate conversion. Faced
by an inquisition panel headed by Ferdinand
himself, he stuck to his faith, and along with

sixty others of his stubborn co-religionists was given six weeks and three days to quit Graz. He realised at once that Prague, formerly the site of all his hopes, was now the only hope remaining to him, and that he must once more throw himself on Tycho's mercy. By mid-October, accompanied by Barbara and his stepdaughter, he was back in the city, exhausted, burning with fever, but knowing he was lucky to have this refuge; as he later wrote, 'God let me be bound with Tycho through an unalterable fate and did not let me be separated from him by the most oppressive hardships.' It is a mark of Rudolf's extraordinary religious tolerance that a man who had been banished from Styria on confessional grounds should be allowed to return to Prague by a Catholic Emperor who, in theory at least, was ruler of the Styrian province that had expelled him as a Lutheran. Kepler and his little family were taken in first by the long-suffering Baron Hoffmann – what, one wonders, was the Baroness's opinion of her husband's unfaltering hospitality? – and later moved in with Tycho and the gang.

It was a hard time all round. Rudolf was still in the throes of dementia, more secretive and paranoid than ever. Tycho was summoned regularly to the palace, sometimes twice or three times a day, to offer astrological advice and, inevitably, to fight for favour among the machinations of an increasingly chaotic court. By now he must have despaired of returning to Benátky. Indeed, in that autumn and winter of 1600 the worm of a general despair seems to have begun to gnaw at him. He was in his middle fifties, a considerable age in those times, and must have been exhausted after more than thirty years of struggling with princes and potentates for the means whereby to fulfil his dream of vindicating the Tychonic system of planetary motion. Although his hated rival Ursus was dead by now, the Ursine legacy lingered, and Kepler was hardly back in Prague before he found himself forced by Tycho to take up again the task of rebutting 'even more clearly and more fully than you have [done] previously Ursus's distorted and dishonest objections to my invention of the new hypothesis,' that is, the Tychonic system. Kepler got to work without enthusiasm on the *Apologia Tychonis contra Ursum*. He was never to finish the book, although the fragment of manuscript he did complete was published in the nineteenth century. Throughout that winter, plagued by a fever he could not shake off, Kepler laboured on the *Apologia*, with little time for his own astronomical concerns, although he did manage to do a little work on the orbits of Mercury, Mars and the moon. The following spring he was back in Graz, trying vainly to secure his wife's confiscated holdings. By the autumn he had returned to Prague. There, Tycho escorted him to the royal palace for a first and, as it would prove, momentous meeting with the Emperor.

Rudolf by now had regained his sanity, such as it was, and Tycho had a proposition to put to him. He would publish, with the help of his assistant Johannes Kepler, a great set of astronomical tables, based on decades of celestial observations and, not incidentally, founded on the Tychonic system, to be called the *Tabulae Rudolphinae*. The Emperor, delighted at the thought of being thus immortalised, readily agreed. In another perhaps uncharacteristic but admirable display of generosity, Tycho stipulated that for the venture to go ahead, Kepler would have to be granted an imperial salary. Again Rudolf nodded assent. Kepler, one surmises, found it hard to know which was the more welcome outcome of this royal meeting, the fact that he was to have a guaranteed wage, or that Tycho had talked himself into a position in which he would find it necessary at last to surrender the observational treasures he had guarded so jealously for so long.

Kepler now suddenly found himself in a favoured position in Tycho's laboratory and in the
Brahe household, no longer an assistant but,
whether it was acknowledged or not, the Dane's
peer, and partner in science. This stellar partnership, however, was not to last for long. On
October 13th, a few days after the meeting with
the Emperor, Tycho went with a friend, one
Councillor Minckwicz, to dine at the Schwarz-
enberg Palace, the home of Peter Vok Ursinus[39]
Rožmberk, where he drank too much wine and
rapidly found himself in urgent need of empty-
ing his bladder. Good manners forbade a guest
to rise from the table before his host had done
so, and Tycho, ever a stickler for the social
niceties, 'felt,' in Kepler's account, 'less concerned for the state of his health than for eti-
quette.' Grimly he waited, but Rožmberk was
either very abstemious or had a prodigious
capacity for liquids, and by the time Tycho
managed to get to the jakes he found he could
not urinate. He returned home, but was still
blocked. Kepler again: 'Uninterrupted insomnia
followed; intestinal fever; and little by little,
delirium. His poor condition was made worse
by his way of eating, from which he could not be

[39] What a baleful portent that name must have sounded to the
Dane!

deterred.' As he lay on what by now he must have known was his deathbed, he begged Kepler, despite his Copernican convictions, to 'present all [Kepler's] demonstration in conformity with [Tycho's] hypothesis,' and repeated over and over, 'like,' according to Kepler, 'a composer creating a song,' the heartbreaking imprecation: 'Let me not seem to have lived in vain!' On October 24th, Kepler continued, 'when his delirium had subsided for a few hours, amid the prayers, tears and efforts of his family to console him, his strength failed and he passed away very peacefully.'[40] He was buried in the Týn church on Old Town Square, with grand ceremonial, his coffin draped in black cloth decorated in gold with the Brahe coat of arms – to this day, probably coincidentally, black and gold are the predominant colours in the interior of this rather forbidding church – his wife following, 'escorted,' according to Kepler's account 'by two distinguished old royal judges, and finally his three daughters, one after the other, each escorted by two noblemen.' Tycho had been ennobled by the Emperor, which meant that Kirsten had at last been 'made an honest woman

---

[40] Medical opinion at the time was that Tycho had died as the result of a kidney stone, but when his body was exhumed in 1901 no stones were found. It is probable that the true cause of death was uraemia.

of', and their children were now fully legitimate, in Bohemia, at least. The Dane would have been gratified by the send-off accorded him by his adopted city. 'The streets were so full of people,' Kepler wrote, 'that those in the procession walked as if between two walls, and the church was so crowded with both nobles and commoners that one could scarcely find room in it.'[41]

Tycho Brahe's tomb still survives in the Týn church, surmounted by a life-sized effigy carved in relief in pinkish-grey marble, and bearing a splendid if slightly obscure epitaph: 'To be rather than to be perceived.'

The end of Tycho's mortal life marked the beginning in earnest of Kepler's professional career. Two days later, with the Dane hardly cold in his grave, imperial secretary Barwitz came with the news that the Emperor had appointed Kepler to succeed Tycho as Imperial Mathematician; even death would not be allowed to delay work on the Rudolphine Tables. Kepler's salary, he was shocked to hear, would be six times less than that which had been paid, or at least

---

[41] F. Marion Crawford's Gothic novel, *The Witch of Prague*, opens with an impressive portrayal of a funeral service in the Týn Church. My copy of the book is a paperback in the 'Dennis Wheatley Library of the Occult' series. Yes, Prague puts one into strange company sometimes.

promised, to Tycho. On the other hand, Kepler now had unrestricted access to Tycho's observations and the use of his instruments, the Emperor having purchased Brahe's astronomical effects from the Brahes for a promised 20,000 florins, although use of the instruments would hardly benefit the bespectacled, double-visioned Kepler. He and Barbara moved from the Hradčany to a house on Vyšehradská Street in the Old Town, not far from the Faust House and opposite the Emmaus Monastery.[42] Despite domestic woes – his marriage was unhappy, his children died – and unseemly squabbles with the Brahes,[43] the years he spent in Prague as Imperial Mathematician were the perigee of Kepler's life, the time when he came nearest to the things he desired, gilt rooms if not gold, and, if not spontaneous applause, at least the odd royal clap on the back. He did some of his greatest work in Prague, on many and diverse subjects, from the orbit of Mars

[42] Now the Czech Academy of Sciences.
[43] Rudolf, of course, did not make good his promise of the 20,000 florins for Tycho's data and instruments, and the Brahe family were reluctant to hand them over to the new Imperial Mathematician. Tycho's assistant, Tengnagel, who had succeeded in having the job of compiling of the *Tabulae Rudolphinae* transferred to him, at twice Kepler's promised salary, demanded the return of Tycho's manuscripts and star charts. Kepler complied, but secretly held back the Mars observations. Give a dog a bone . . .

through the functioning of the human eye to the
structure of snowflakes, and completed the first
of his masterpieces of theoretical science, the
justifiably titled *Astronomia nova*. He kept Tycho's dying plea in mind, and gave the Dane his
due recognition, but he could not vindicate Tycho's misconceived system. As one biographer
neatly puts it, '[h]istory celebrates the Copernican Revolution, not the Tychonic Revolution.'

In 1608 Rudolf was forced to abdicate as
Emperor, and after Rudolf came the deluge, in
which Kepler, along with any prospect of peace
in Counter-Reformation Europe, was swept up
and washed away. By the winter of 1611,
Prague was in chaos. Troops under the command, so-called, of Archduke Leopold V,
Bishop of Passau, whom Rudolf had engaged
in a hare-brained plot to regain power, ran riot
in the city, doing the things that an undisci-
plined soldiery always does, and clashing in
running, bloody battles with gangs of Bohemian vigilantes. In his house in the New Town,
Kepler, labouring to uncover the secret harmony of the universe, could look down from
the window of his workroom on the scenes of
mayhem and rapine in the streets round about.
Meanwhile on the Hradčany the atmosphere in
the royal palace 'was thick with madness and

ruin'[44] as Rudolf's final piece of lunacy ended in his being stripped of all power and his hated brother seizing the Bohemian throne. In April Kepler had his own fall from grace, when the impossibility of life in Prague forced him to accept a teaching post at a school in Linz in Upper Austria. The Imperial Mathematician was once more a schoolmaster. There was worse to come when, in June, Barbara died of fever. Despite his genuine grief for this woman who had shared so many of life's vicissitudes, Kepler married again, a little more happily this time, although the children of his second marriage were also to die, as his and Barbara's had. Then, in 1615, a charge of witchcraft was brought against his mother, and he spent the next six years – yes, six years – engaged in her legal defence. He got her off, but she died a few months later. Through all these trials and troubles Kepler never ceased to work at astronomy. As the world around him collapsed into the disorder and horror of religious warfare, he became more and more obsessed with the quest for celestial harmony, turning now, as a true Pythagorean, to music as a model. On May 15th, 1618, completing

---

[44] This fine phrase is from Ferguson's *The Nobleman and His Housedog*.

the final stages of one of his key books, the *Harmonice mundi*, he discovered the third law of planetary motion, the 'harmonic law', defining the relationship between the orbits of the planets and their distances from the sun. He was exultant, and at the end of the *Harmonice* composed a paean of gratitude to his God: 'O You who by the light of nature arouse in us a longing for the light of grace . . . I give thanks to You, Lord Creator . . .'

On May 23rd, eight days after Kepler had discovered his third law, a crowd of a hundred or so Protestant nobles forced their way into the Chancellery of Rudolf's palace to protest at the revocation of Rudolf's 'Letter of Majesty' – which had guaranteed religious tolerance in the province – and the attempts by Rudolf's Habsburg heirs to suppress the Bohemian church, founded at such bloody cost by Jan Hus. Acting in the usual way of the devout when they have been slighted, they seized on two Catholic councillors, Jaroslav Bořita z Martinic and Vilém Slavata, and threw them and their secretary, Filip Fabricius, out of the Chancellery's eastern window. The three clung on to the sill, but the leader of the Protestants, Count Thurn, beat on their fingers with the hilt of his sword until they let go. Luckily for the victims, the moat far below the window was clogged with sewage, so that they had a relatively soft landing. This was, as every schoolboy used to know, the Second Defenestration of Prague, and the beginning of the Thirty Years War.[45] The Emperor Matthias died the following year, and the crown passed to his nephew, Ferdinand II, the Jesuit-trained bigot who had personally exiled Kepler and his co-religionists from Graz in 1600. The Bohemian Estates promptly rebelled, and invited Frederick V, the Elector Palatine, to become King of Bohemia. In 1613 Frederick had married the Princess Elizabeth, daughter of James I of England. Europe

---

[45] Praguers have a distressing fondness for throwing people from high places. In 1393 the fourth King Wenceslas, obviously not half so good as his dynastic ancestor and namesake, had the Vicar-General of the Archdiocese of Prague, Jan Nepomucky – later canonised as St John of Nepomuk – thrown from the Charles Bridge and drowned in the Vltava. Later, in 1419, after the death of Wenceslas, followers of the religious radical Jan Hus flung the Mayor of Prague and his councillors to their deaths from the windows of the New Town Hall, with no piles of dung to break their fall. Leaping forward – if that is not too tasteless a formulation, given the topic – to the twentieth century, on the morning of March 10th, 1948, the Czech Foreign Minister, Jan Masaryk, a liberal who had tried to limit communist power in the new coalition government, was found dead in the courtyard beneath the open window of the Foreign Ministry; it was assumed he had committed suicide in face of the prospect of the Stalinisation of his country, but suspicions persist that he did not jump but was pushed. It is understandable therefore, that in the fateful month of August 1968, there were many who feared that the Russians would do in Prague as the Praguers do and thrust the reformist First Secretary, Alexander Dubček, from some conveniently high elevation.

John Banville

had high hopes for the golden couple, who 'have something of the air of a Shakespearean hero and heroine.'[46] Their fabulous castle at Heidelberg, 'with its gardens and grottoes, its water organs and singing statues', was a rival for Rudolf's Hradčany palace and 'a citadel of advanced seventeenth-century culture.'[47] Elizabeth was a young woman of wide learning,[48] while her husband was described by the English Ambassador as 'much beyond his years religious, wise, active, and valiant'. The couple debated carefully the offer of the Bohemian

---

[46] Frances Yates, *The Rosicrucian Enlightenment*. The Lady Elizabeth was a keen theatregoer, and at Christmastide in 1612, the King's Men, Shakespeare's company, presented *The Tempest* for the couple's delight on their betrothal night. Yates notes that some scholars have suggested that the nuptial masque in the play had been added to the original version especially for the occasion. And on the wedding night, February 14th, 1613, a masque, with words by Thomas Campion and produced by Inigo Jones, was presented at the banqueting house at Whitehall before the newlyweds and the court. Yates quotes a charming chorus:

> *Advance your chorall motions now,*
> *You musick-loving lights,*
> *This night concludes the Nuptiall vow,*
> *Make this the best of nights;*
> *So bravely crowne it with your beames,*
> *That it may live in fame,*
> *So long as Rhenus or the Thames*
> *Are knowne by either name.*

Alas, the magical union of Rhine and Thames was not to endure.
[47] Ibid., p 41.
[48] Her daughter, another Elizabeth, was to be the dedicatee of Descartes' *Principia*.

crown, consulting among others the Arch-
bishop of Canterbury, who urged acceptance,
and Frederick's mother, who implored him to
say no. However, Frederick the zealous Protestant considered that he had been divinely
called, and on September 27th, 1619, he and
Elizabeth set out with their eldest son, Prince
Henry, for Prague. Much of Protestant Europe
rejoiced, while England considered that the
'only Phoenix of the world', Queen Elizabeth
I, was about to return in the form of her
namesake. The coronation of the couple in St
Vitus's Cathedral was, as Frances Yates remarks, 'the last great public ceremony to be
sponsored by the Bohemian church'.

Bohemia believed its new King and Queen
would be the saviours of the country's autonomy
and the religious freedoms which had been one of
the more solid aspects of Rudolf's mystico-ma-
gical reign. But Bohemia was dreadfully mistaken. It had put its faith in Elizabeth's father,
James of England, whom they believed would
champion their cause, with military might if
necessary. James, however, in awe of the Habsburgs, was against the Bohemian adventure, and
behind the scenes busied himself in disowning his
daughter and her husband. Nor did the German
Protestant princes come forward with the sup-

port that might have been expected of them. Meanwhile the Catholics were massing their forces, and on November 8th, 1620, Frederick's army was utterly defeated at the Battle of White Mountain, fought at Bíla Hora just outside Prague. The 'Winter King' fled with his wife to The Hague. After the rout, the Habsburgs exacted a frightful revenge on the Bohemian Protestants. The following year, on the morning of June 21st, twenty-seven leaders of the Czech Protestants, including nobles, knights and burghers, were beheaded on the Old Town Square by the Prague executioner, Jan Mydlář. One of those who died on that day of infamy was kindly old Jan Jesenský, Rudolf's doctor and later Rector of Prague University, who had acted as arbitrator in Kepler's negotiations over the terms of his contract with Tycho Brahe. The heads of the twenty-seven victims were impaled on spikes on the Charles Bridge, where they remained for a decade, until Swedish forces entered the city in 1631 – Brahe's Scandinavian heart would have swelled with justly vindictive pride – and removed them for burial in the Týn church. Ripellino in *Magic Prague* sees that terrible day as emblematic of the city's miseries down the centuries, and rages in particular against Mydlář the executioner, condemning him to the inferno: '*In ignem aeternum, in ignem aeternum!*'

Kepler spent the final years of his life wandering restlessly back and forth across war-ravaged southern Europe, seeking support first from the Duke of Württemberg, which was refused on religious grounds, and, more successfully, from the Bohemian general Albrecht Wallenstein, Duke of Friedland and Mecklenburg and Prince of Sagan, who had scored a notable victory by repulsing an invasion of north Germany by Christian IV of Denmark – once again Tycho in his grave must have bridled with satisfaction – and who was almost as strong a believer in the influence of the stars on the fortunes of men as the Emperor Rudolf had been. Wallenstein lured Kepler to Sagan in 1628 with the promise of a house and a grant of 1,000 florins a year, as well as a printing press on which he might publish his own books, in return for which rewards Kepler would act as the general's official astrologer. The printing press was particularly welcome, as publishing was more difficult than ever in those years of endless war, and Kepler had a pet project – his last, as it happened – that he was determined to put into print. This was *Somnium*, the world's first work of science fiction, a twenty-eight-page fantasy of a trip to the Moon. In it, the narrator visits Uraniborg and learns Danish in order to communicate with Tycho and his assistants, after which he travels to the Moon and gives an account of how the Earth and the planets appear from a lunar perspective.

Somnium was an unintentionally prophetic title. Printing of the book was still under way in October 1630 when Kepler set out on his last, brief wanderings. From Sagan he travelled 450 kilometres south to Linz – surely stopping off at Prague – in a vain effort to collect back pay from his teaching post there. From Linz he rode nearly the same distance north again all the way to Leipzig to sell his wares at the autumn book fair in the city. He had shipped ahead nearly 150 of his own books, including sixteen copies of the *Tabulae Rudolphinae*, which, despite Tengnagel's attempt to take them over, Kepler had finally completed in 1624; they were, as later scientific scholars have attested, a miracle of thoroughness and accuracy, and in them Kepler paid due regard to the man who had made them possible, Tycho Brahe. When the fair was over Kepler rode another three hundred kilometres south to Regensburg, where the Diet was meeting to settle the succession of the Emperor Ferdinand's son, another Ferdinand, who had conspired to depose Kepler's patron Wallenstein from command of the imperial armies. Kepler hoped to beard the Emperor and extract from him monies that were still owing to him as Imperial Mathematician, a title which he still held, worthless though it was. He arrived in Regensburg on November 2nd, riding a broken-down nag, and lodged at the house of an old friend, Hillebrand Billig. There he fell into a fever, and died two weeks later. He was a month short of his sixtieth birthday. He had already prepared his own epitaph, which, like everything this endearing, bizarre and prodigiously gifted creature wrote about himself, contains a hint of amusement and self-mockery:

> *I measured the heavens, now the earth's shadows I measure.*
> *Skybound my mind, earthbound my body rests.*

5

SNAPSHOTS

Summer, sometime in the middle of the 1990s. The city is hot and smoky, and seems to gasp, as if in distressed relief at having survived the terrible decades, so I fancifully think. It is my first visit since the Velvet Revolution – that journalist's formulation, which I have never heard a Praguer employ, has definitely begun to irritate – and I cannot help but search for signs of change everywhere. I am staying at U Páva ('At the Peacock'), a pleasant little hotel close by the Charles Bridge in Malá Strana. At night from the wide-open window of my room I have an uninterrupted view over the treetops of Vojan Park to the Castle on its hill, glaringly floodlit. I switch off the bedside lamp to get the full effect. The floodlighting is a post-1989 innovation, surely? The communists would have regarded such a show of unashamed consumption of the city's electricity supply as a typical piece of Westernised decadence, and probably they would have been right. Standing at the window in the moth-dusted darkness I am struck by how little like a castle the Castle is, with its long, blank, fortress wall studded with row upon row of tiny square windows and not a turret in sight and the spires of St Vitus's thrusting their witch's fingernails into the sky in what seems a gesture of frozen hysteria. Václav Havel is the President now. The fact is hard to credit, even yet. It is as if Kafka's K. had suddenly been welcomed into the Castle by a smiling Kramm and told that with immediate effect he will cease to be a lowly land surveyor and instead assume the leadership of the realm. I try to picture this playwright, admirer of Beckett and Ionesco, sitting in his neat blue suit at a desk in Rudolf's palace, poring over documents of state. Havel himself is fully alive to the absurd dimension of his rise to power. In a speech in Jerusalem shortly after his inauguration he expressed, with an almost jaunty frankness, his feelings of incongruousness – of being, even, an imposter.

I am the kind of person who would not be in the least surprised if, in the very middle of my Presidency, I were to be summoned and led off to stand trial before some shadowy tribunal, or taken straight to some quarry to break rocks. Nor would I be surprised if I were to suddenly hear the reveille and wake up in my prison cell, and then, with great bemusement, proceed to tell my fellow-prisoners everything that had happened to me in the past six months. The lower I am, the more proper my place seems; and the higher I am the stronger my suspicion is that there has been some mistake.

If he were indeed to be apprehended, no doubt the nameless authorities would in their mordantly witty way send a pair of clapped-out actors to make the arrest, perhaps even dressing them up in frock coats and non-collapsible top hats.

At midnight suddenly the floodlights are switched off. It is a shock, especially as it happens without a sound; somehow, so vast a disillumination should be accompanied by a peal of bells, or a thunder-crack, or at least the amplified sizzle of a gigantic flashbulb. Unnerved, I fumble my way into bed and feel like pulling the blankets over my head. When my eyes have accustomed themselves to the dark I see that one of the Castle windows, just one, is still lit. Someone must be working late. I suppose by association with my thoughts of Havel I recall a fragment from Beckett, 'the little lights of man . . .' Comforted, I close my eyes. There is a part of the self that is always a child.

I was in Prague to attend a literary festival, with a side trip to Bratislava where I would address a gathering of academics. My friend Zdeněk, the writer, had collected me from the airport in his brand-new green car which his daughter Jindra, with whom he lodges, insists is blue. In his late seventies, Zdeněk, who loves to drive, loves his car; the silliness of this attachment amuses him. In the driving seat, though, he is very serious, the wheel held firmly with both hands at the top and his head thrust so far forward his forehead almost touches the windscreen. On that sunny afternoon we drove through pleasant suburbs that could have been the outskirts to any European city. I ask about property prices. He shrugs. They are going up, like everything else. He and Jindra have to share a tiny apartment, even though Jindra has an important job in Havel's office. I tell him about my unsettling experience with the Castle floodlights, and the solitary window that remained lit. He laughs, and says that of course that will have been Jindra's office: she always works late. The coincidence strikes me as a little bit of Prague's old magic, and I am charmed. Jindra's window is suddenly an Archimedean lever powerful enough to lift the night itself a momentous inch or two.

U Páva, my recently renovated hotel, is on a narrow hillside street, U lužického semináře.[49] The reception desk just inside the front door was a little booth with a high counter from behind which I was greeted by the manageress, a handsome blonde woman who took me for a German. Zdeněk, who had insisted on carrying my suitcase from the car, spoke to her in Czech and she immediately switched to English. Yet again I was plunged in shame for my lack of languages. Zdeněk departed, saying he would pick me up that evening and he and Jindra would take me to dinner. The manageress, whose behind I could not help admiring, led me up the narrow stairs. There were hunting prints on the wall . . . Suddenly, now, this second, remembering those prints, I realise that it was U Páva which I used as the model for a hotel in a novel I wrote in the late 1990s, a hotel not in Prague but in Porto Venere, a seaside village in Liguria, where one of my characters had gone to commit suicide.

[49] U lužického semináře is named after a sixteenth-century seminary founded exclusively for the education of postulants from the Lužice region in the eastern part of the country, which had its own Slavic language, since lost. Now you know.

Fiction is a strange, voracious business, and no respecter of the uniqueness of places or persons.

The opening session of the Writers' Festival takes place in a small, extremely hot room, filled with cigarette smoke, over a restaurant on the Old Town Square directly opposite the Town Hall with its astronomical clock.[50] The clock tower is remarkable not only for its brightly painted dials but for the life-sized figures that adorn it, among them Death, Vanity, Greed, Archangel, and head-shaking Turk. Praguers have an enduring predilection for statues, figurines and automata of all kinds, from the *Jezulátko*, the famous Infant of Prague – of which I had a treasured miniature, gilt version when I was a child –

---

[50] The clock, completed in 1410 by Mikoláš of Kadaň, was rebuilt in 1490 by a master clocksmith named Hanuš, who did such a fine job that the town councillors, fearful that he would make a replica elsewhere, had the unfortunate craftsman blinded. The mechanism of the clock as it is today is the work of Jan Táborský, who, from 1552, spent twenty years perfecting it. When the clock chimes the hour, the figure of Death pulls on a rope with his right hand, while lifting and inverting the hourglass he carries in his left. Two doors above the clock face then creak open and a number of figures including the twelve Apostles, led by St Peter, emerge and do their round. The doors close, a cock crows and the hour is chimed. The clock not only tells the time but also shows the position of the Sun and the Moon as they circle the Earth fixed at the centre of the world – Kepler must have snickered when he first passed under the tower. Beneath the clock is another, rather pretty dial, painted in 1846 by Josef Mánes, showing the signs of the Zodiac and pictorial representations of the months of the year. The clock is a popular tourist attraction. That is an understatement.

through various miraculous Madonnas, at least one of them black, to Karel Čapek's robots[51] and the monstrous Golem, the alarming morphs that people the animated films of the great Jan Švank-majer, the numerous puppet theatres still flour-ishing in the city – most of them, alas, mere tourist traps now – and, of course, uncanniest of all, Kafka's *odradek*, a star-shaped creature resembling a spool of thread which propels itself – himself? – about the house of the nameless narrator of the fragment 'A Problem for the Father of the Family', emitting a laugh that sounds 'like the rustling of fallen leaves'. Ripelli-no, of course, that connoisseur of the uncanny, is fascinated by Prague's fascination with the unhu-man. He is particularly taken with the Jezulátko, that eerie godling with its globe and jewelled crown, 'a wax doll dressed in silk, gold brocade or other costly materials depending on the season and displayed in the Baroque Carmelite Church of Our Lady Victorious', which was brought from Spain by Polyxena of Lobkowicz in 1628, during Rudolf's reign. 'If the massive Golem . . . was a harbinger of disorders and disasters,' Ripellino writes, 'the Jezulátko – an

---

[51] Čapek in his play *R.U.R.* coined the word 'robot' from the Czech term *robota*, the labour owed by a vassal to his feudal overlord, and the Old Slavonic *rob*, meaning slave.

exquisite rag doll and model of delicate fabrics –
was a salubrious balm cheering the spirits of the
disheartened, a physician for both body and
soul.' There follows a splendid example of the
Ripellinonian *non sequitur*: 'And the fact that the
principal patron of the dark church where it lies
and where the mummies of the Carmelite Order's
protectors lie in sumptuous open coffins was the
cruel Spanish general Baltazar de Marradas (who
commissions the Jezulátko in his death throes
from the sculptress Flavia Santini in Julius
Zeyer's legend 'Inultus' [1895]) is of scant sig-
nificance.'

But I must return, however unwilling, from
these statuesque frolics to the sober business of
the Prague Writers' Festival.

Despite the organisers' best efforts, the opening
session is happily chaotic. People wander in and
out of the smoke-filled stifling room, not only
audience members but the participating writers,
too. The atmosphere is at once manic and vague.
I discover to my consternation that I am due to
chair one of the discussions. The topic has something – I never quite succeeded in discovering
exactly what – to do with East–West literary
influences. I have no notes, have made no preparations, and since the majority of the panel of
speakers are Czech, I spend most of the hour, the

very long hour, floundering in linguistic confusion, which the simultaneous translation in my headphones only serves to intensify. One of the writers, a grumpy chain-smoker with a brigand's heavy black moustache, objects at length to the fatuousness of the topic under discussion, and indeed, if I understand him, to the very idea of the festival itself. He speaks of the great, gone days of *samizdat* – much of which, I am fascinated to learn, was financed by George Soros – then lapses into a grumpy silence. I call, in some desperation, on a Hungarian member of the panel to comment. He and I have a previous, brief acquaintance, but he seems to have forgotten that he ever met me, or perhaps it is that when we met – in Budapest, was it, or Vienna? – I somehow managed to offend him. He talks about a novel I have not read by a writer I do not know, then looks to me in polite expectation of an informed reply. At this point the chain-smoker gets to his feet with a sigh and ambles out, to the lavatory, I assume, but in fact he was never to return. Close to panic now, I attempt to 'throw the discussion open to the floor', and endure a couple of minutes of shuffling silence as the audience sits and gazes at me in what seems barely suppressed resentment. At last someone asks a question about censorship in the bad old days, which only serves to provoke more shifting of feet and clearing of throats. Into the restive silence I remark gingerly that the present strength of Czech literature – I mentioned Klíma, Hrabal, Michal Ajvaz – would seem to indicate that writers had not only survived the years of communist rule, but had triumphed. And then, with the horrified fascination of a fat man feeling himself begin to fall slowly, helplessly and catastrophically down a steep flight of stairs, I hear my voice, seemingly of its own volition, asking if perhaps Gore Vidal's assertion that Hollywood never destroyed anyone who was worth saving might be adapted to Soviet communism and Czech writers . . . ? The rest of the session passes for me in a hot haze of cringing embarrassment. At last, the hour up and my penance served, I throw off my headphones and with ringing ears make a shamed escape into the square, where, sure enough, the Turk is shaking his head at me in mournful reproval, Death turns up his hourglass and pulls on his rope, and the chimes of the clock toll the death knell of my brief, but not brief enough, career as an arbiter of Czech literature.

In the afternoon, seeking balm for my still burning blushes, I pay a visit to the Old Jewish Cemetery, a pilgrimage every traveller to Prague must make. I last saw it under snow, one deserted winter twilight in the 1980s. On this sweltering afternoon it is a Dantesque scene, thronged with tourists shuffling along specified walkways between the jumbled, moss-grown tombstones, the estimated number of which varies between 12,000 and 20,000, depending on which guidebook you choose to trust. The oldest stone, from 1439, is that of Rabbi Avigdor Kar, or Kara, or Karo; the latest, marking the grave of Moses Beck, is dated May 17th, 1787. Buried here also are two of the leading Jews of the Emperor Rudolf's time, the financier Mordechai Meisl, richest Praguer of his day,[52] and Rabbi Judah Loew ben Bezalel (?1520–1609), one of the greatest Jewish scholars of the Renaissance, and Prague's Chief Rabbi from 1597 until his death. Rabbi Loew is the subject of many legends, especially those featuring Yossel the Golem, the giant clay man whom Loew is said to have fashioned from a lump of earth, as God created Adam from the dust of Elohim. The story goes that in the year 1580 a certain friar by the name of Thaddeus, a fanatical anti-Semite, raised

---

[52] Meisl was a great philanthropist, and built three synagogues – one of which bears his name – public baths, a hospital, and the Jewish Town Hall, overlooking the Cemetery, which has a Hebrew clock the hands of which turn backwards, a detail not missed by Apollinaire in his hallucinatory poem 'Zone'.

accusations of superstitious rituals and blood sacrifices against the Prague Jews. Rabbi Loew appealed to Yahweh for help, and in a dream was instructed to create the Golem as a protector of the faithful against the Christian mob. He summoned his son-in-law, Isaac ben Simon, and a disciple, the Levite Yakob ben Chaim Sasson, to represent respectively the elements of fire and water, while the Rabbi himself was the element of air; the Golem, of course, would be the final element, earth. After the three had performed the intricate ceremony of religious purification they went to the banks of the Vltava at midnight and kneaded a human figure from river clay. First Rabbi Loew instructed Isaac the priest to walk seven times around the Golem, starting from the right, chanting Psalms and reciting magical formulas and letter combinations as he went, then Yakob the Levite was ordered to circle the figure another seven times, starting from the left. After this, Rabbi Loew himself circled the Golem, which, feeling the effects of the three elements, began to glow with the heat of life. Finally, the Rabbi inserted a *shem hameforash*, a slip of paper on which was written the unutterable name of God, under the Golem's tongue, and the creature rose to his feet, a living homunculus ready to do his master's bidding.

The Hebrew word *golem*,[53] meaning rudiment, embryo, or merely earthly 'substance', appears in Psalm 139:

> *My substance was not hid from thee, when I was made in secret, and curiously wrought in the lowest parts of the earth.*
>
> *Thine eyes did see my substance, yet being unperfect; and in thy book all my members were written, which in continuance were fashioned, when as yet there was none of them.*

Rabbi Loew was a great scriptural scholar, and also an adept of the Cabala, a mystical philosophy based on visionary writings which originated among the Jews in thirteenth-century Spain, and which had a widespread vogue during the Emperor Rudolf's reign. Cabalistic teachings reached well beyond the Ghetto, and were a strong influence in Neoplatonism, for instance, and even on the magical thinking of John Dee. Rudolf, needless to say, was deeply interested, and in 1592 summoned Rabbi Loew to the Hradčany and had a lengthy, secret meeting alone with him.[54] How

[53] Wearing his Professor of Useless Information hat, Ripellino informs us that '[I]n the Talmud a woman who has not yet conceived and a jug requiring polishing are termed *golem*.'

[54] Rudolf was remarkably tolerant of the Jews; a number of his closest advisers were Jewish, and he is known to have consulted the wealthy Mordechai Meisl for advice on the imperial finances, and most probably touched him for the odd substantial loan, too.

one longs to have a record of that conversation.

The Cabala might be said to be the underground religion of the Jews. It is a creation myth and a Jewish form of Messianism, and incorporates numerology and a complex science of alphabetical combinations known as *gematria*. The legend of the Golem's creation speaks of complex rituals in which permutations of the Tetragrammaton, the four-letter symbol of God's name, was of paramount importance. From this and other hints it seems clear that the Golem story is a debased, popular version of a Cabalistic creation myth. How peculiar, then, that the never less than dogmatic Ripellino should insist that the legend of Prague's Golem 'goes back no further than Romanticism', making its appearance first in a five-volume collection of tall tales and anecdotes, in German, not Yiddish, entitled *Sippurim*, published by Wolf Pascheles in the middle of the nineteenth century. There is no mention of the Golem, Ripellino points out, in David Gans's 1592 chronicle of the Jews of Prague, *Zamach David* ('Descendants of David'), nor in a biography of Rabbi Loew published in 1718.

However, Ripellino is speaking only of the *written* legend. Yossel the Golem is as old as the Prague Ghetto. There had been Jews in the city from at least the tenth century; indeed,

Ghetto lore had it that the Jews had come to Prague after the destruction of the Temple of Jerusalem. Following the Third Lateran Council of 1179, a papal ordinance directed that a wall should be built to separate the Ghetto from the southern, Christian, parts of the city. Despite persecution and anathema, the Ghetto flourished, stretching from the north side of the Old Town Square up to the banks of the Vltava. In 1781 the Emperor Joseph II abolished the law under which Jews were confined to the Ghetto. The imperial aim was not to liberate the Jews, however, but to assimilate them fully into Christian society as a means of destroying their culture and their languages – Hebrew and Yiddish were banned, and the Jews were forced to Germanise their names. By the beginning of the nineteenth century only ten per cent of the population of the Ghetto was Jewish, and in 1850 the area was turned into a municipal district and renamed Josefov. However, as the *Blue Guide* pointedly observes, the reforming Emperor 'would not, perhaps, have entirely appreciated the honour, for the district was by now a festering slum . . .' In the 1890s, despite protests from architects and artists, most of the hovels and warrens of alleyways had been cleared to make way for the somewhat soulless, Haussmannian avenues of the present-day Josefov, although some of the finest buildings were spared, including the Old-New Synagogue and Meisl's splendid Town Hall. Surprisingly, perhaps, the Nazis too, after the invasion of Czechoslovakia, decided to preserve the surviving monuments, with the intention of turning them into a Museum of Jewry which would be an ironic commemoration of a race soon, they thought, to be extinct. During the Nazi occupation nearly 80,000 Jews were murdered, and today only a tiny community of Orthodox Jews remains in the area. More Jews would have died if not for the underground efforts of brave and decent people such as my friend Zdeněk, who in the 1990s was honoured by Israel for his wartime work on behalf of Prague's Jewish population.[55]

Yossel the Golem, this kosher version of Frankenstein's monster, had both a benign and a bad side. Having thwarted Friar Thaddeus, he took to patrolling the streets and back lanes of the Ghetto, keeping guard over the houses of the poor so that no malignant *goy* could come creeping in to hide the bodies of Christian children in Jewish homes. One night he surprised the butcher

---

[55] It was futile to press Zdeněk for details of what he did for the Jews; he would merely smile and shake his head and wave a dismissive hand. To be brave and not to boast of it is bravery squared.

Havlíček carrying the corpse of a baby hidden in the belly of a slaughtered pig into the house of Mordechai Meisl, to whom he was indebted, with the intention of denouncing the banker as a ritual murderer. There came, however, that Friday evening when Yossel went on the rampage. Rabbi Loew had forgotten to give him his Sabbath eve instructions for next day, and in his boredom Yossel ran amok, stamping everything in his path to pieces, until the Rabbi was called upon to quell his monster. Eventually, like a pet that refuses to be house-trained, the Golem had to go. One night at the beginning of 1593 – the designation of a particular year is a nice touch on the part of the legend-maker – Rabbi Loew instructed Yossel to sleep not in his own bed in the Rabbi's house but to spend the night in the attic of the Old-New Synagogue. Two hours after midnight, Rabbi Loew, with his henchmen Isaac and Yakob, climbed to the loft where the Golem lay sleeping. First the Rabbi removed the *shem* from under the creature's tongue, then the three men performed the same ceremony by which they had brought the Golem to life, but this time in reverse, and by morning all that was left of poor Yossel was a pile of clay.

The Rabbi himself met a more poetic end, when he bent to savour the perfume of a rose his granddaughter had presented to him, only to discover that Death himself was hiding among the petals. A better way to go, certainly, than the ignominious end that befell, literally, his Polish colleague, the famous miracle-working Rabbi Elijah of Chelm, called Israel Ba'al Shem Tov, who had his own Golem. When the latter's time was up, Rabbi Elijah chose to destroy him by erasing the first letter of the word *emet* graven on the creature's brow, leaving the word *met*, that is, death. However, the Rabbi made the mistake of ordering the Golem to erase the letter himself; when he did so, he turned back at once into a load of clay which promptly collapsed on Rabbi Elijah, crushing him.

In the Josefov today there is little of the atmosphere of the Ghetto left, apart from an oppressive sense of absence, of emptiness, despite the poet Nezval's assertion that Rabbi Loew's *shem* is still here, 'under the tongue of all things, even of the pavement, though made of the same stone with which all Prague is paved.'[56] Only in the imagination does the old world live on. Ripellino, lover of twilight and crowded streets, prowls the place in his fancy. 'I feel I lived in that Ghetto long ago; I see myself as a Chagallesque Jew at

[56] Ripellino, p. 109.

Succoth with an *etrog*, a yellow cedar branch, in my hand or at Chanukkah, lighting an eight-armed menorah with a *shammes* candle, or as one of the *shammosim* in the many synagogues, or wandering through the foul, *gespenstisch* darkness of the narrow streets.'

Zdeněk insists on driving me to Bratislava, where I shall attend my academic conference. He arranges for us to motor down in the morning, and after lunch he will drive back to Prague; this is a round trip of six hundred kilometres. I insist it will be excessive kindness, but Jindra laughs and says her father is not being kind, only seizing the opportunity to take a good, long drive. The summer day is soft and still; by noon the sun will scorch the roof of Zdeněk's beloved green, or blue, car. At a crossroads we stop and Zdeněk points across the fields to his family's farm, confiscated from his father in 1948 and given back to the family after 1989; Zdeněk shakes his head, bemused that he should have lived to see such wonders.[57] At the border with Slovakia

[57] 'After 1989 all properties nationalized by the revolution (factories, hotels, rental apartments, land, forests) were returned to their former owners (or more precisely, to their children or grandchildren); the procedure was called *restitution*: it required only that a person declare himself owner to the legal authorities, and after a year during which his claim might be contested, the restitution became irrevocable. That judicial simplification allowed for a good

there is a passport control booth. I ask Zdeněk what he thinks of the separation of Czechoslovakia into two states, and he shrugs; the Czech Republic is the richer half, but the Slovaks wanted their autonomy, and they got it. Later, in Bratislava, I shall be given a different account, in which the wily Czech Prime Minister, Václav Klaus – whom Zdeněk, in tones of high, icy irony, refers to always as '*Mister* Klaus' – tricked the Slovaks into a bad deal because he wanted to be shot of them and their economic problems. As we drive through the Slovak countryside, there are farmers and their families in the fields making hay; not since my earliest childhood have I seen a hand-made haystack. The scene might have been painted by Millais, or one of the less cloying Socialist Realists.

Bratislava is not Prague. The Old Town, in the centre, is handsome and charming, but all around, the city, at least in the time that I was there, resembled a sprawling construction site. After lunch I was driven into the countryside, to a nineteenth-century mock-Gothic castle, the entrance to which was guarded by a pair of mighty

deal of fraud, but it did avoid inheritance disputes, lawsuits, appeals, and thus brought about, in an astonishingly short time, the rebirth of a class society with a bourgeoisie that was rich, entrepreneurial, and positioned to set the national economy going' (Milan Kundera, *Ignorance*).

steel gates that opened before me in slow, menacing silence. In communist times the place had
been a retreat for authors favoured by the State,
that is, apparatchiks and hacks. My third-floor
bedroom was enormous, dotted here and there
with looming items of black-lacquered furniture.
A tall window looked down with what seemed a
melancholy gaze upon a scene of heat-hazed
woodland and a pond with ducks. I spent a
restless night, lying stiff as a board in my shiny
black bed. In the morning my friend Igor, one of
the organisers of the conference, cheerfully en-
quired if I had slept peacefully, and when I said
no he chuckled and said he was not surprised:
previous guests in the Black Room had included
Khrushchev, Brezhnev, and a crazed writer, one
of the last of the privileged pre-eighty-niners,
who had leapt from the window to a messy death
beside the duck pond. Shakily I descended to the
conference room and delivered my paper on
Synge and the Aran Islands; when I was finished,
a Canadian academic with a mien of steely ambi-
tion attacked me for what he claimed to believe
was my rabid Irish nationalist views. Not a
pleasant experience, at ten in the morning after
a night spent in a bed once occupied by Leonid
Brezhnev.

That evening, back in Bratislava, I was invited

to a party, where I spent an agreeable half hour chatting to a writer and translator, I shall call him Mr H., who had just published his translation of a Modernist Irish classic into Czech, a task that had taken twenty years of loving labour. He complained that before 'the changes', that is, before 1989, when the State controlled publishing, only the finest, most edifying works of Western literature were translated, but nowadays every kind of American trash was being allowed into the country. Afterwards I mentioned this conversation to Igor, who chuckled again – I was learning to interpret Igor's many modulations of chuckle – and said that certainly Mr H. would know all about State publishing policies under the communists, since he had been the official Censor.

When the conference ended Zdeněk came down again from Prague to collect me. I told him how another man I had met at that party – oiled black hair *en brosse*, thick spectacles, a peculiar, silvery suit that seemed made of tinfoil, and a manner that inevitably made me think of Big Phil, the Man Who Knows the Inside Story – had informed me, with the air of one who is merely repeating a matter of common knowledge, that in the final months before the 1989 revolution, Havel in prison had been conniving with the Czech intelli-

gence service to take over the Presidency when
Husák's régime fell, as everyone had known it
very soon would. Zdeněk, however, was adamant: such a thing was not possible. I did not
persist, but privately I thought that even if it had
been true, I would not have thought any less of the
President. Politics is politics, even if you are a
playwright of the Theatre of the Absurd. By now
we were on the outskirts of Prague. As we drove
down through a smoky industrial suburb, Zdeněk
pointed out the spot at a bend in a road where the
Gestapo chief Reinhard Heydrich had been assassinated by Czech partisans in 1942; in reprisal for
his killing the Nazis razed the coal-mining village
of Lidice, twenty kilometres northwest of Prague,
and shot 184 men, the entire male population of
the village, the oldest a man of eighty-four, the
youngest a boy of fourteen. In the following days
German troops buried the charred remains of the
village under soil, and the name Lidice was ex-
punged from the map. Today, the memorial
erected on the site in 1947 is one of the most
frequently visited war memorials in the Czech
Republic.

The Writers' Festival is closing, and I am invited
to a British Council party. It is held in a handsome house – not the Embassy, but someone's

home – on one of those leafy streets off behind the Castle, that part of Prague where the tourists do not go, and which many Praguers consider to be the true heart of their city. I had tried to avoid the party – the novels of Malcolm Bradbury have jaundiced me for ever against such occasion – but my friend Claudio Magris, writer, Germanist and Triestino, who also has been taking part in the Festival, says I must be there, 'to meet Gold-stücker'. I do not know who this Goldstücker is, and am not eager to be introduced to yet another new person at the end of a week of mostly baffling encounters with voluble stran-gers. However, my host and hostess – the Smith-Jones, let us call them – turn out to be remarkably unlike the usual run of British Councillors, being funny, irreverent, and discerning in their choice of wines.[58] The party is small, a couple of dozen guests sitting about on chairs and sofas in what appears to be the Smith-Jones's living room – I find a child's sock under my chair – so that it is possible to engage in something like real con-versation. I am recounting my Slovakian adven-ture, Black Room and all, to an attractive young woman whose name I did not manage to catch

[58] The matter of the well-chosen wine will be appreciated by those readers who have attended a British Council party anywhere in the world.

but who laughs rather prettily at my shameless exaggerations, showing an interesting fleck of lipstick on her upper incisors, when Claudio grasps me by the arm and drags me away. 'Come come come, you must meet him, come!'

Professor Doctor Eduard Goldstücker is a handsome man with a large, squarish face, eyes of a clear, marine blue, and hands that are also squarish and large; he is in his early eighties, and looks twenty years younger. He sits on a sofa in the middle of the room, those big hands resting on his knees, looking before him with such a tranquil gaze, his head tilted slightly upward, that for a moment I wonder if he might be blind. Quite the contrary is the case, as I discover: I think I have never met anyone more sharp-eyed. There is another quality he possesses that is harder to describe. He somehow contrives to fill with extraordinary exactitude the space that he inhabits; compared to him, I realise, most people seem to be rattling around in the ill-fitting envelope of themselves, like astronauts in their space suits. I am introduced, and Goldstücker invites me to sit beside him; he is, he says, a great admirer of Irish literature. He points to a painting on the wall opposite where we sit – he has been studying this picture, which explains the upward tilt of his gaze as I approached – an unremarkable landscape, with polders, and a rainbow arched over a misty, dull green distance. He had been wondering, he said, if it might be an English scene, for it reminded him of the Sussex Downs. I stared, I suppose, and he produced what I can only describe as a basilisk smile: eyes electric with amusement, nostrils flared, the lips compressed and turned not upward but down. He had taught at Sussex University throughout most of the 1970s, having fled Czechoslovakia the day before the Russian invasion in August, 1968, and later settled in Britain. 'Hence,' he said with arch self-mockery, 'my impeccable English.'

Over the following hour or so, Goldstücker told me his story, and since then I have filled in some of the details from other sources. It strikes me as being, in certain significant and appalling ways, the story of Prague itself in the second half of the twentieth century. He was born in the village of Podbiel, in Slovakia, in 1913, the son of a Jewish timber merchant. In 1931 he moved to Prague, to study German and French literature. At university he became the leader of a communist student group, and in 1933 joined the Czech Communist Party. He taught in a secondary school until 1939, when he and his wife escaped the German occupation and fled to England via Poland and Sweden; the members of his family who remained behind were to die in Auschwitz. In London Goldstücker edited the journal *Mladé Ceskoslovensko* (*Young Czechoslovakia*). Later, in 1943, he worked in the Foreign Ministry of the Czechoslovak government in exile in London, and in 1944 became cultural attaché at the Czech embassy in Paris. After the war he returned to Prague and became a civil servant at the Foreign Ministry, returning to London as attaché at the embassy there from 1947 to 1949. Following the communist takeover in 1948 his career as a diplomat flourished briefly. He was appointed Ambassador to Israel in 1950, and to Sweden in 1951. It was in 1951, however, that Stalin ordered a purge of Jews from the Communist Party. Along with a number of others, Goldstücker was rounded up in December 1951 and taken to the headquarters of the secret police, where he was kept in almost total isolation and subjected to constant interrogation.

'When I first arrived at police headquarters, out near the airport,' he told me, 'I asked them why I had been arrested, and on what charges. The chief interrogator smiled at me – such an ironic smile! – and said, *That's not for us to tell you, but for you to tell us.*' He laughed, remembering it. Then, glancing sideways at me, he held up a hand. 'Please,' he said, laughing again, 'please don't mention Kafka.' The interrogations went on around the clock, three teams of questioners taking eight-hour shifts. Luckily, he said, he had been something of a mathematician at school, and was able to keep himself sane by working out equations in his head. What did they want from him, I asked, what did they expect him to confess to? 'That I was an enemy agent bent on undermining the régime. They were preparing me for a show trial, and in order for my court confession to sound to some degree authentic, I must produce the evidence against myself. You see?' There was a brief silence, and then he answered the question I dared not ask. 'Oh, of course,' he said, 'I did "confess". There was no other way out.'

The show trial took place a year and a half after his arrest. Everything was rehearsed. 'It was theatre,' he said, 'a kind of grotesque and meticulously prepared performance. I was presented with a text, on which were listed the court's questions, and my answers. If I did not keep to the text, strayed from it in any way, the trial would have been called off, and I would have been sent back to the secret police for the process to begin all over again.' His lawyer had given him a single piece of advice – do not use swear words before the bench – and then went into court and opened the case for the defence by saying that the 'supreme punishment', that is, the death sentence, was being demanded for his client, and that 'no doubt he deserves it.' However, since he was not a leader of the 'conspiracy' the court might find it in its heart to be lenient. Big-hearted as the judges were, they retired for the night to consider their verdict. 'The trial had lasted,' Goldstücker said, 'from nine in the morning until four in the afternoon. Then, from four until nine the following morning, I had to live with the distinct possibility of being sentenced to death and executed right away.' He smiled again. 'Doctor Johnson was right: the prospect of being hanged in the morning does concentrate the mind.'

He was spared the death penalty, and sentenced to life imprisonment instead. He was sent to the uranium mines, where he spent two and a half years digging radioactive material with his bare hands. 'I cannot understand,' he said, 'why I have not died of cancer long ago.' There were periods when he could move about only on all fours, even when work had ended for the day. In all this time, he was not aware that Stalin had died at the beginning of 1953. Khrushchev, prior to the momentous 20th Congress of the Communist Party in Moscow in 1955, at which he secretly denounced Stalin, had begun to release prisoners from the Gulag. The Czech authorities saw which way the Siberian wind was blowing, and started their own discreet programme of releases. By Christmas 1955, the same court which had almost sentenced him to be hanged changed their verdict, decided the charges against Goldstücker had been illegal, and ordered that he should be set free immediately. 'The governor of the prison where I was held called me to his office,' Goldstücker said. 'He was obviously embarrassed – I remember how he kept nervously moving documents about on his desk – and warned that it might be some time before I could be released. Of course, all my hopes collapsed at once, for this was just the kind of cruel trick they liked to play, these people: tell you that you would be set free, then delay your release for years. *Yes*, the governor went on, *it could take two or three hours before we can get you out of here.*' Goldstücker was studying the watercolour landscape again. 'In that moment I realised,' he said, almost dreamily, 'that I was dealing with a man who was – how shall I say? – who was not human. If he thought that, after the years of interrogation and imprisonment that I had endured, I would consider three hours to be *some time*, then no, he was not a human being, as I understand being human.'

After his release he found a position in the philosophy faculty of the Charles University, later becoming Professor of German Literature there, and eventually was appointed Deputy Vice Chancellor. In May 1963 he organised the legendary Kafka Conference at Liblice Castle, which paved the way for Kafka's rehabilitation in Czechoslovakia. In the years that followed he busied himself with academic work, was a representative briefly on the National Assembly, and in January 1968 became President of the Czechoslovak Association of Writers and one of the promoters of the Prague Spring. That springtime proved a short season, as we know. 'The Russian invasion had just taken place, and my wife and I had fled to Vienna,' Goldstücker said, 'when I received a telephone call from a journalist in England, telling me that the University of Sussex wished to offer me a teaching post. I accepted, of course. But do you know, I did not catch the journalist's name, and to this day I cannot say who my benefactor was.'

It is an indication of the strangeness of those times in Prague that Goldstücker returned the following year, for a few days only, during which he was sworn in as a member of the Czech National Council. He wanted to remain in Prague, but the Husák government claimed to have uncovered a planned coup against it by dissidents, of whom Goldstücker was one. He returned to Sussex, and in 1974, in his absence, his membership of the Czech Communist Party was revoked. He was happy in England, he said, or at least not unhappy. Eventually, in 1989, Czech history took another of its recurring twenty-year turns when Husák and his Calibans fell and Václav Havel came to power. At once Goldstücker contacted the new Czech government to say that he wished to come back to Prague. The answer he received was equivocal: it might be some time before he could be allowed to return . . . He had, after all, he was reminded, been an active communist during the Novotný régime. It was not until his daughter in Prague became friendly with the daughter of the Havel government's Foreign Minister that he was at last given permission to return – 'to come,' he said, 'home.'

And what, I asked him, was his attitude to communism now? 'Oh, I am still a socialist,' he said, 'I never lost that faith. The people with the power were bad – more than bad – but the system was not.'

I kept in touch with Goldstücker, and some years later I arranged, with the sponsorship of the Goethe Institute, for him to come to Dublin. He wrote to say that he looked forward to the visit, set for the following spring, but warned that I should realise that for a man of his age the Prague winter would be a 'hazardous undertaking'. As it happened, he did not make it through the autumn. On October 24th, 2000, the Goethe Institute telephoned me to relay the news that Professor Goldstücker had died the previous day. It is not too much to say that, for me, an essential part of Europe, and of Prague in particular, died with him.

EPILOGUE – THE DELUGE

It is said that the name of the Vltava river is made up of two words from the lost language of the Celts, *vlt*, meaning wild, and *va*, meaning water. In normal times the visitor to Prague would think this an unlikely derivation. The great, broad river – in places it is a third of a kilometre wide – meanders its way through the city, skirting an island here, there spilling gently over a weir, placid, it would appear, as a village stream. More than one of Prague's disenchanted writers have seen in it a symbol of what they consider the shallowness of the people who live along its banks; Gustav Meyrink, for instance, sourly observed that a foreign fool might think the Vltava as mighty as the Mississippi, but in fact is it 'only four millimetres deep and full of leeches'. But T.S. Eliot got it right when, in the *Four Quartets*, he declared:

. . . I think that the river
Is a strong brown god – sullen, untamed and
*   intractable,*
Patient to some degree, at first recognised as a
*   frontier;*
Useful, untrustworthy, as a conveyor of commerce;
Then only a problem confronting the builder of
*   bridges.*
The problem once solved, the brown god is almost
*   forgotten*
By the dwellers in cities – ever, however, implac-
*   able,*
Keeping his seasons and rages, destroyer, reminder
Of what men choose to forget.

Certainly, a large number of Praguers had forgotten just what the river could do when its back
was up. There have been many floods in the city
over the past hundred years – in 1890 two arches
of the Charles Bridge were washed away – but
none so terrible as the cataclysm of the summer of
2002. On the night of August 8th–9th, after a
week of torrential rains, a vast surge of waters
gathered in southern Bohemia and began to
race toward the capital, swamping and in some
cases destroying villages and towns along the
way: Český Krumlov, Český Budějovice, Písek,
Strakonice, Štěchovice . . . Prague was unpre-

pared for what was coming. By the time the waters began to subside on August 14th, an entire district of the city, the former industrial centre and lately somewhat yuppified Karlín, had been virtually destroyed, half the metro stations were closed – and will remain so indefinitely – precious old buildings had been damaged, some beyond repair, and tourist figures had fallen by fifty per cent. The cost of repairing the water-logged fabric of the city would run into billions of Czech crowns, and no one could say who would end up footing the bill. It was a European disaster.

I visited Prague a month after the floods had subsided. As a rule I avoid places where natural disasters have occurred; even when I walk through the ruins of Pompeii or Herculaneum, beautiful, fascinating and moving though these ruined cities are, I feel uncomfortably as if I have gatecrashed a wake. In such places Mme de Staël's identification of the predicament of the tourist – 'What I see bores me, what I don't see worries me' – becomes intensified to the level of a moral reprehension. Over the years I have spent many happy days in this city, so accommodating of the *chodec* – stroller, *flâneur* – but after such damage, what is to be my attitude now, and how should I comport myself?

I arrive at the evening rush hour, but there is little traffic. The city's almost Venetian silence, which I register at the start of every visit as if I were hearing it, not-hearing it, for the first time – this, more than the Mitteleuropan ambience or the ravishing architecture, is what, for me, gives the city its unique character and is part of the explanation for the enduring mysteriousness of the place. On a film set, the sound recordist at the end of a scene will record what is called a wild track, a minute or so of silence to keep as background should part of the scene need to be re-dubbed; in Prague, it always seems to me that someone has forgotten to do the wild track, and that behind even the loudest scenes of festival or protest or just everyday business, there is a depthless emptiness. But the silence is different now, in this amber-coloured, waterlogged September. The Venice it suggests is not a Venice on water, but under it.

One needs to know something of the successive defeats and invasions the city has suffered through the centuries to appreciate the full extent of the shock that Praguers felt as they cowered before the raging waters of the Vltava that August. It was the White Mountain all over again. Here was another assault to be resisted, not from without, this time, but from within. Suddenly, the

thing in their midst that they had 'almost forgotten' literally rose up against them. After the
first torrents had raged through the city – one
eyewitness I spoke to described seeing a forty-
foot container, torn from the back of a jugger-
naut, hurtling down the river on a sixty-kilo-
metre-an-hour surge of waters – people in the city
told of their incredulity and growing horror as
day after day they watched the river's levels
continue to rise; an Irish diplomat described to
me how each morning as she walked to her
embassy office in Malá Strana she would look
down successive side streets and see the fringe of
dirty water inching its way inexorably upwards.
At its highest, the flood reached a height of some
four metres; one could still see the high-water
mark on the houses, shops and restaurants of
Malá Strana.

Most of the bridges were still closed to all
modes of conveyance save trams and taxis, the
ban enforced by soldiers and armed police man-
ning roadblocks. Traffic on the main thorough-
fares near the river was even more chaotic than
usual; one commuter said that travelling by tram
in the city now reminded her of the public transport system in Calcutta: 'The trams are so
crowded, people are practically sitting on the
roofs!' Yet the sense I had was not of panic or

desperation or a jostling for safety, but of a great sadness, rather. At the turning of every street corner something seemed to breathe in my face, an exhausted, soundless sigh out of a shadowed past. It was as if the flood waters, coursing through the catacomb of cellars and underground passageways beneath the city, had stirred something ancient and elemental in Prague's very foundations. I felt as if I had come to visit a sometime lover and found her beautiful as ever, but aged, and melancholy, and fearful of the future.

For Praguers, there was no romance in any of this. The city might sound, and smell, like Venice, but this cistern silence and rank odour would attract no visitors. Businesses had been ruined; some of the biggest and most expensive hotels were closed, and would stay closed, possibly for years; precious murals were washed off the inner walls of Renaissance buildings in Malá Strana; for children going to school, for workers going to factory or office, finding means of transport was a nightmare. Yet as everyone in the city, native or foreign, will attest, Praguers showed magnificent spirit and capability in dealing with the crisis. All the same, the question remained: Who would pay? A flood tax proposed by the government was voted down by parliamentarians who suspected a ploy to raise taxes in general. On Wenceslas Square students were selling bricks from buildings demolished by the floods in an effort to raise funds for flood repair. The gesture seemed heartbreaking, but heartening, too. Prague would survive. Prague always survives.

AFTER-IMAGES

There is so much I have not said, so much I have not told about my love affair, its intensities and lamentable intermittences, with the city on the Vltava. I am thinking of the stifling evening at the Charles Bridge when I was pickpocketed by a tiny, thin, quite beautiful child-woman, whom I chased – to my surprise and obscure shame – and who, when cornered, pulled open her summer dress, under which she wore only a skimpy set of flowered underwear, and grinned fiercely, showing white teeth and a wad of well-chewed gum, and invited me in guttural Czech to search her, while a fellow who was most likely her pimp stood a little way off, looking at his nails, no doubt with my wallet already stowed in his back pocket. I am thinking of a diplomatic occasion organised for me in a residence on one of those bosky streets behind Hradčany, to which I turned up hopelessly overdressed in sober suit and tie and starched shirt, while the Ambassador and his people were in shirt sleeves, cheerfully unbuttoned, and ready to talk all night about the fascinations of Prague and Praguer affairs. I am thinking about a dinner in an upstairs restaurant in Malá Strana below the Castle steps with Zdeněk and his daughter Jindra, and how Zdeněk told such wonderful stories against himself, and how much we laughed. I am thinking of myself standing on a street corner in the Josefov one deserted summer afternoon, with not a soul in sight in any of the four directions in which I could look, and how happy I felt suddenly, for no earthly reason, except that I was alive, and in Prague, and for a little while free of myself, and that the moment was precious precisely because it would not come again. *How easily the blown banners change to wings*, Wallace Stevens writes of another city, in another time. Yes, how easily . . . Prague, as Kafka said, has claws, and does not let go. I shall leave the last word to Ripellino, my inspiration and tirelessly enthusiastic cicerone. 'When I seek another word for mystery,' he writes, 'the only word I can find is Prague. She is dark and melancholy as a comet; her beauty is like the sensation of fire, winding and slanted as in the anamorphoses of the Mannerists, with a lugubrious aura of decay, a smirk of eternal disillusionment.'

ACKNOWLEDGEMENTS

As the reader will certainly know by now, I owe a large debt to Angelo Maria Ripellino's *Magic Prague*, translated by David Newton Marinelli and edited by Michael Henry Heim (Macmillan, London, 1994), which itself, I am glad to note, relies heavily on the writings of others.

All Seifert quotations are from *The Selected Poetry of Jaroslav Seifert*, translated by Ewald Osers, edited and with additional translations by George Gibian (New York, 1986).

The quotations on pages 36–7 are from Johan Huizinga's *The Autumn of the Middle Ages*, translated by Rodney J. Payton and Ulrich Mammitzsch (Chicago, 1996).

The Kafka quotations on pages 40–41 are from *The Trial*, translated by Idris Parry (London, 1994). There is an eccentric but charming little book, *Franz Kafka and Prague*, by Harald Salfellner (third edition, Prague, 2002), which contains many curious and fascinating details of the writer's life and his feelings for and against Prague, as well as numerous apt quotations from the diaries and letters. The quotations on pages 10, 24 and 25 are taken from Salfellner's book.

John Banville

For biographical details of the photographer Josef Sudek, and other valuable information and artistic assessment of his work, I am grateful to Dr Zdeněk Kirschner, whose *Josef Sudek* (New York, 1993) contains a fine collection of the artist's pictures, with an illuminating introduction, personal remembrances, and notes. I must also mention *Sudek* by Sonja Bullaty and Angelo Lomeo, with an introduction by Anna Fárová (New York, 1986), one of the finest studies devoted to Sudek's art, with superb reproductions. A number of Sudek's remarks quoted in my text are taken from her preface.

For the meditation on bridges on pages 76–7, see *Poetry, Language, Thought*, by Martin Heidegger, translated by Albert Hofstadter (New York, 1971).

For the passages devoted to the Emperor Rudolf, I am indebted to R.J.W. Evans, whose *Rudolf II and His World* (Oxford, 1973) is a comprehensive, subtle, and sympathetic portrait of this fascinating man and the city on which he stamped his character indelibly.

Frances Yates has written extensively on John Dee, especially in *Theatre of the World* (London, 1969). For more on the brief reign of Ferdinand and Elizabeth, the unfortunate Winter King and his queen, see Yates's *The Rosicrucian Enlightenment*

(London, 1972), and *Shakespeare's Last Plays: A New Approach* (London, 1975).

The standard modern life of Tycho Brahe is *The Lord of Uraniborg: A Biography of Tycho Brahe*, by Victor E. Thoren (Cambridge, 1990). In her informative and entertaining study of Brahe and his turbulent collaboration with Johannes Kepler, *The Nobleman and His Housedog – Tycho Brahe and Johannes Kepler: The Strange Partnership that Revolutionised Science* (London, 2002), Kitty Ferguson seems to have leaned not unlightly, as have I, on Thoren's authoritative monograph.

Milan Kundera's *Ignorance* is translated from the French by Linda Asher (London, 2002). Jan Neruda's *Prague Tales* is translated by Michael Henry Heim (London, 1993).

There are dozens of available guidebooks to Prague, but for much practical information, and memory-jogs, I turned frequently to *Blue Guide: Prague*, by Michael Jacobs *et alii* (London, 1999), and *Eyewitness Travel Guides: Prague*, by Vladimír Soukup *et alii* (London, 1994).

For further copyright details please see page iv.

My thanks to Deirdre Bourke, Liz Calder, H.E. Joseph Hayes, Tereza Límanová, Justin Quinn, Anthony Sheil. I wish also to thank Beatrice Monti Rezzori, director of the Santa Maddalena Foundation at Donnini, in Tuscany, and her assistant, Alessandra Gnecchi Ruscone. It was in the very beautiful and tranquil surroundings of Santa Maddalena that I completed my Prague journey. *Grazie per tutti*.

In special memory of Jindřiška Dušková.

A NOTE ON THE TYPE

The text of this book is set in Linotype Sabon,
named after the type founder, Jacques Sabon. It
was designed by Jan Tschichold and jointly
developed by Linotype, Monotype and Stempel,
in response to a need for a typeface to be available
in identical form for mechanical hot metal
composition and hand composition using foundry
type. Tschichold based his design for Sabon
roman on a fount engraved by Garamond, and Sabon
italic on a fount by Granjon. It was first used
in 1966 and has proved an enduring modern
classic.

HRADČANY
U BRUSNICE
CHOTKOVA
KLÁROV
FORTRESS OF HRADČANY
GOLDEN L.
VIKÁRSKÁ
ST. VITUS CATHEDRAL
LETENSKÁ
NOVÝ SVĚT
NERUDOVA
ST. NICHOLAS
LORETÁNSKÁ
ÚVOZ
KARMELITSKÁ
MALÁ STRANA
STRAHOV MONASTERY
KAMPA ISLAND
PETŘÍNSKÉ GARDENS
ÚJEZD
MOST
STRAHOVSKÁ
N
HOLEČKOVA